MASTERING BOUNDARIES

THE MOST **POWERFUL** RELATIONSHIP TOOL TO ADVANCE SELF LOVE, MARRIAGE, FRIENDSHIPS, FAMILY, DATING AND BEYOND

BY JENNY MORROW, MS, MFT

COPYRIGHT NOTICE

Mastering Boundaries: The Most Powerful Relationship Tool to Advance Self Love, Marriage, Friendships, Family, Dating and Beyond

Relationship Education is an imprint of Hazelnut Publishing

Author Photograph by Kayli Pendleton

ISBN 979-8-9892225-4-4 (paperback)

ISBN: 979-8-9892225-5-1 (hardback)

ISBN 979-8-9892225-3-7 (ebook)

DISCLAIMER

The information in this book is intended for educational and topic interest purposes only. The suggestions and advice written in this book are the opinions of the author only, and are not intended to be a substitute for therapy, psychological counseling, abuse support, addiction help, legal advice, financial advice, or any other type or form of professional help.

This book is not intended to diagnose, assess, or treat. This book is not intended to serve as the basis for your relationship decisions. You should seek the services of competent professionals if you need any expert assistance for your specific situations.

The author and publisher disclaim all and any responsibility or liability resulting from your actions. The author and publisher specifically disclaim any responsibility for any liability, loss, risk, or any physical, psychological, emotional, personal, legal, financial damages, or otherwise, that may be incurred as a

CONTENTS

ABOUT THE AUTHOR

Jenny Morrow is an 18-year Marriage Therapist, Relationship Coach, and advanced relationship educator. She is the founder of Advanced Relationship Coaching, a personal coaching model designed to help individuals and couples view and create change through the lens of relationships with self and others. This model was inspired by Jenny's work in the fields of Marriage Therapy, Relationship Coaching, Life Coaching, Yoga, Psychology, Mindfulness, and Visioneering.

Jenny is married to Bryce Bauer. Bryce is the creator of the Hierarchy of Relationship Needs, which Jenny writes about in this book. He has a background that includes over 13 years as an International Coaching Federation Certified (ICF) Life Coach and four years of specialized training in relationship coaching. Before his work as a life coach and relationship coach, he spent years working with adult men and women in inpatient treatment facilities and wilderness therapy. Bryce is the author of the book *Men In Marriage: How To Show Up In Your Most Important Relationship*.

Jenny and Bryce have over 30 years of combined research, learning, and education. They have sat in over 20,000 sessions with private clients. Together, they run a relationship education company that offers courses, coaching, workshops, retreats, and coach training.

If you would like to learn more, go to:

www.jennymorrow.com

This book is dedicated to all those who have granted me the privilege to encounter and explore the art and science of boundaries, including my clients, family, friends, mentors, and my most constant and courageous boundary-exploration partner—my husband, Bryce.

To Get The Most Out Of This Book

This book is for those who want a comprehensive course on mastering boundaries and creating advanced relationships. To supplement the learning in this book register for the Mastering Boundaries Book Bonus that includes:

- A 60-Min. video where author, Jenny Morrow, answers questions from readers like yourself.

- Downloads of the charts and images used in this book, such as the Four Quadrants of Masking and the Advanced Relationship Blueprint.

- A library of Advanced Relationship videos from Jenny and her husband, Bryce, delivered straight to your inbox, including:

- How To Share Your Needs In A Relationship
- Attachment Styles 101
- 3 Ways That Self Improvement is BLOCKING Your Growth
- Too Good To Leave & Too Bad To Stay. How To Navigate Relationship Ambivalence

To register for your book bonus, use the QR code or go to **www.jennymorrow.com/bookbonus**

As soon as you register, you will emailed access to the entire book bonus features and video library for free!

Chapter 1
THE JOURNEY OF MASTERING BOUNDARIES

INTRODUCTION

After nearly two decades of helping people advance in their relationships with themselves and others, I believe that boundaries are the most essential relationship tool to learn and master.

What are boundaries? What makes the difference between effective and ineffective boundaries? This book provides a comprehensive study of boundaries. It illustrates a clear picture of how boundaries differ at different levels of relationship needs, and explores what it takes to master boundaries at each level of relationship fulfillment.

By initiating a journey of self-discovery and learning to establish boundaries in harmony with your genuine desires, you unlock new opportunities that were previously beyond reach.

In this way, boundaries become the most powerful tool for creating the life and relationships you desire.

My 20-year journey into mastering boundaries has led to remarkable transformations in my own life, including the evolution of my work, the transition out of a high-demand religion, and the co-creation of a deeply fulfilling marriage.

Other areas in which you can apply boundary mastery to achieve desired results include health, friendships, money, parenting, business, and more.

This book represents a culmination of extensive research, education, practical experience from my own journey, and insights gleaned from client work. Welcome to the fascinating and transformative world of boundaries!

PURPOSE OF THIS BOOK

This book is designed to equip you with the comprehensive knowledge needed to master boundaries in your own life. It may be particularly valuable if you encounter any of the following experiences:

- Feel small, unimportant, insignificant, or unworthy to create the life or relationships you desire.
- Wonder why your efforts to improve things aren't working.
- Feel trapped, lonely, or destined to "just survive."
- Notice guilt, anxiety, or confusion when you try to set a boundary.

- Find yourself in frustrating patterns of conflict.
- Feel like a victim in your life or in a relationship.
- Believe you need to fix yourself or someone else.
- Feel like you have to hide parts of who you really are.
- Wonder why you're doing all the "right" things but can't create the life or relationships you want.
- Attempt boundaries, only to feel like it makes things worse.
- Often give time and resources to others, but rarely have enough for yourself.
- Work in a helping profession.
- Want to create a life and relationships that are more authentic.
- Feel ready to build deeper and more fulfilling relationships.

WHAT ARE BOUNDARIES?

The word "boundary" is frequently used in our modern vernacular, and while the word appears to be straightforward, it encompasses a wide range of meanings and applications across various contexts.

Boundaries serve as a protective barrier, such as the walls of a house or a warrior's shield.

Boundaries also denote distinctions between different entities. For instance, my first name, Jenny, is a boundary that sets me apart from other Morrows, which is my last name. Similarly, the borders around Colorado differentiate it from surrounding states in the US, such as Utah or Wyoming.

Boundaries also help direct creativity, development, and expertise in a specific field. For example, the boundaries of a yoga pose instruct the placement of hands, elbows, legs, and feet to form a particular shape that can be practiced to increase strength and flexibility.

In the context of this book, I define boundaries as ***the tools and interventions used to fulfill relationship needs***, encompassing not only the need for safety but also the higher-level needs of partnership and relational expansion.

This comprehensive definition incorporates all facets of boundaries—including protection, identifying distinctions, and amplifying creative support. The specific type of boundary you apply at any given moment will depend on the level of relationship need you are working to fulfill.

In this book, I will introduce The Hierarchy of Relationship Needs as a framework that you can use to distinguish between levels of relationship fulfillment and when to use what type of boundary.

WHY MASTERING BOUNDARIES MATTERS

Many people are taught to engage in what I call *traditional boundaries*. These are boundaries oriented solely toward survival and formed from shadows of the past. Traditional boundaries lead to traditional outcomes, such as:

- **Traditional Relationships & Marriages**: These relationships maintain unspoken desires and unexplored power dynamics. This leads to unproductive cycles of conflict, including aggressive arguments, battles over who is right and wrong or, on the flip side, passive responses that, while designed to keep the peace, lead to disconnection, boredom, and flatness. The patterns enabled by these relationships generate anxiety, loneliness, and other negative emotions. Over time this results in unfulfilling relationships, divorce, and dissatisfaction with commitment.

- **Traditional Body Aesthetics:** In this experience, one's focus becomes conforming to societal or cultural beauty standards, which prompts constant attempts to change one's appearance through excessive exercise, diets, styles, or plastic surgery. Alternatively, one may feel that true beauty is unattainable and neglect opportunities for joyful and healthy aesthetic expression.

- **Traditional Jobs & Careers:** Here work is a means to an end, with the goal being to make money and survive. The mindset of these jobs includes living for the weekend and eagerly anticipating retirement. On the flip side, work is viewed as a "rat race" to be avoided for an alternative lifestyle that prioritizes freedom but misses opportunities to connect with meaningful work.

- **Traditional Spirituality:** This type of spirituality outsources spiritual and moral authority to dogmas, gurus, experts, or spiritual leaders who claim exclusive truth or act as intermediaries to a higher power. On one side is avoidance of logical evidence if it discounts a particular leader or spiritual view, and on the other, avoidance of any experience that lacks quantifiable, rational, or intellectual purpose, including distancing oneself from art, imagination, story, or engagement with mystery, awe, and wonder, leading to a life that feels robotic, empty, or meaningless.

- **Traditional Financial Life:** This is characterized by constant financial scarcity and the need to sacrifice honest, aligned desires to get ahead or break even. Alternatively, if the bank accounts are full, they cannot be enjoyed or appreciated in a genuine way.

- **Traditional Health:** Here, the body and mind are constantly on high alert and hypervigilant, fighting against various perceived threats and making one feel unsafe in their body and world. On the flip side is disconnection from one's body and health, where one dismisses cues of imbalance and ignores the body's needs for sleep, healthy food, exercise, or medical attention.

While it's not uncommon to utilize traditional boundaries, they are inherently limiting, and at some point in your personal development, you will be ready to move beyond a traditional approach to creating the life and relationships you want. When that happens, the motivation to learn—what I call *advanced boundaries*—begins to materialize.

Advanced boundaries are sourced in the present and are designed to support both surviving and thriving. When you shift from a traditional boundary approach to an advanced boundary approach, you will begin to notice:

- Deeper, more authentic connections
- A greater sense of confidence
- More palpable love
- Enhanced leadership abilities
- Improved safety and security
- Genuine playfulness and adventure
- More expansive freedom
- An enriched sense of purpose
- Increased experiences of joy
- Greater influence in relationships
- More complete relaxation and rest

The first step in transitioning from traditional to advanced boundaries is learning the Hierarchy of Relationship Needs. This framework will help you differentiate between the different relationship needs and the type of boundaries that are required to fulfill each one.

Chapter 2
THE HIERARCHY OF RELATIONSHIP NEEDS

The Hierarchy of Relationship Needs was created and designed by my husband, Bryce Bauer (Bauer, 2021). Bryce has given me full permission to use the model and to interpret, teach, and share it. All of the interpretations, teachings, and writings about the model in this book are my own.

The Hierarchy of Relationship Needs, often referred to in this book as the "hierarchy" is a five-tier model that lays out the five levels of relationship needs.

When Bryce first showed me this model, I felt so excited. After sitting in over 14,000 client sessions, I thought, "This nails it!" The Hierarchy of Relationship Needs takes what I've observed over the years and presents a visual image illustrating the order through which relationship needs arise, are met, and fulfilled.

Because boundary work varies at each stage of relationship development, I now frequently utilize this model with students and clients. This enables them to customize their boundary work to the level of relationship need they are working to fulfill.

WHAT TYPES OF RELATIONSHIPS CAN BENEFIT?

The Hierarchy of Relationship Needs applies to all relationships, including your relationship with yourself, and all relationships can benefit from understanding this model.

When thinking about your relationships, imagine the ripples that cascade out when you plop a rock into the water.

First, there's the initial impact, where the rock hits the water—the center of the ripples. This center represents the most important relationship in your life—your relationship with yourself.

I call this the most important relationship because it is the relationship that is always with you, from birth to death, every day and every night of your life. You live moment to moment with yourself more than you will ever live with anyone else. Every situation, experience, thought, emotion, and sensation that you encounter in your lifetime is filtered through your relationship with yourself.

From there, your experience of relationship ripples outward, starting with those that you are most attached to, dependent on, and around most frequently.

If you are married or have a primary partner, this is often the next ring in the circle. For most people, a primary partner is someone you plan a life with, combine finances with, and sleep next to every night.

Saying that you want to live a great life but you are okay with having a mediocre primary partnership is not far from believing that you can create a great life while having a mediocre relationship with yourself.

It doesn't really work, and this continues to be true, though less and less so, as you move out through the layers of the other rings in the circle, including the rings that represent your relationships with your children, parents, friends, siblings, business partners, neighbors, co-workers, and so on.

The reality is that developing advanced relationships takes time, energy, and resources. Ultimately, this isn't a problem because the payoff is so high, but it does mean that you will need to prioritize and decide which relationships will get what amounts of your energy, time, and attention.

HOW THE HIERARCHY OF RELATIONSHIP NEEDS IS SET UP

The Hierarchy of Relationship Needs is a hierarchy, meaning there is a particular order in which the five levels of relationship needs are addressed and fulfilled.

The image of the hierarchy is a pyramid, with the first and most fundamental need at the base of the pyramid, and each subsequent need adding a new layer to the structure. The pyramid illustrates that you can only build up particular layers of relationship development after first fulfilling preceding needs.

While the concept is illustrated as a hierarchy, it is not meant to be a rigid design that excludes specific situations, personalities, and contexts that may include nuance and, at times, unexpected ways that relationship needs get experienced, desired, and fulfilled.

Even though each level is clearly delineated, there are transition areas where one's focus begins to shift from the fulfillment of one specific need to the arising of the next. During these transition phases, preceding needs do not need to be one hundred percent fulfilled before the desire for the next level need arises.

You may also observe that when there is a rupture in a preceding need, you can maintain some fulfillment of subsequent needs while addressing the work to resolve and repair the ruptured level.

It's also important to note that certain intentions and choices can impact the fulfillment and rupture of multiple relationship needs at once.

I will provide boundary examples for each level of relationship fulfillment. This will allow you to perceive the notable distinctions in boundary work as you progress from one level of relationship need to the next.

Chapter 3
RELATIONSHIP NEED – LEVEL ONE

PHYSICAL SAFETY is the first level of relationship need. The subtitle for physical safety is *My Body*.

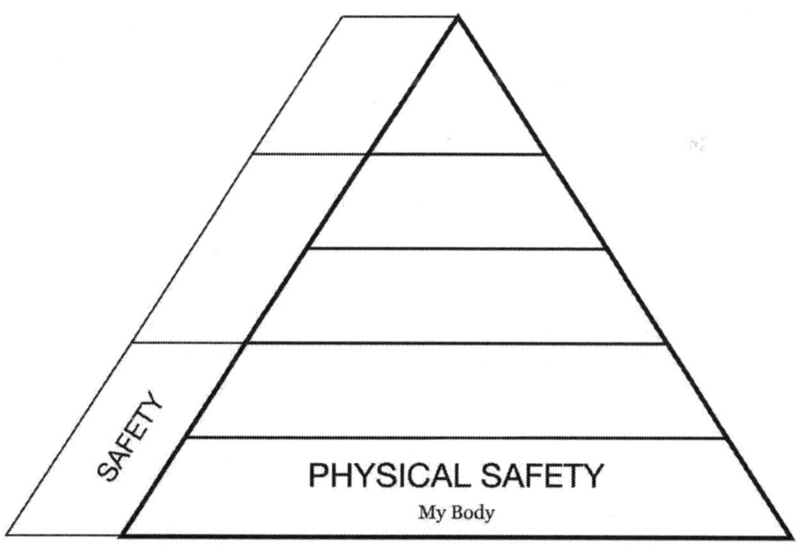

Figure 1 – Hierarchy of Relationship Needs Level 1 (Bauer, 2021)

Physical safety pertains to the question: *"How safe is my body in the presence of this relationship?"*

Here, you are assessing and addressing your physical well-being within a relationship. This level focuses specifically on the security of one's body, including safety and access to resources.

The word ***My*** in the subtitle ***My Body*** is a reminder that, ultimately, it is your individual responsibility to secure your physical safety. Although you may wish and envision that those around you will prioritize your safety and advocate for it, this may not always be a reality.

If you are unwilling to care for your own safety as much as you expect or hope others will do so, you might find yourself in a continuous struggle, wondering why you can never get your needs for physical safety met.

Depending on the situation, engaging in couple counseling sessions can potentially cause more harm than good in cases of physical abuse. At the same time, research suggests that couple therapy may be a viable treatment in select situations. (Karakurt et al., 2016)

For this reason, I recommend seeking professional support from someone knowledgeable in violence issues to help you lay out a plan for individual work and when and how to integrate relationship work in a particular relationship, if ever.

While education and professional support can help you learn how to assess and create physical safety, it is ultimately your responsibility to acknowledge your experience, make decisions about the boundaries you will apply, and follow through on holding those boundaries.

If you have any children or dependents, you are also responsible for assessing and securing their physical safety.

TWO ASPECTS OF PHYSICAL SAFETY

Violations of physical safety can be classified into two primary categories: ***Body Safety*** and ***Resource Security***.

Physical Safety Category #1: Body Safety

In this context, you are examining whether any aspect of a relationship – such as conflicts, another person's moods, mental health conditions, addictions, choices, and so on – raises any concerns about the physical safety of your body. The fundamental question to ask yourself is, "Does this relationship jeopardize the physical safety of my body?"

Physical and sexual violence are the main perpetrators that impede your body's safety within a relationship. If you or your dependents experience any form of physical or sexual violence, it violates the need for physical safety.

Furthermore, additional indicators that can suggest a lack of body safety in a relationship include the following:

- Pressure or force to ingest dangerous substances, such as being given a date rape drug, or undue pressure to take any mind-altering substance.

- Physical restraint such as being locked in a room.
- Pressure or force to engage in physical or sexual activities that are dangerous or high-risk.
- Undue pressure or force to engage in touch.
- An experience of being in a sexual relationship with someone who is secretly engaging in high-risk sexual relationships with others or who hides the fact that they have a sexually transmitted infection.
- Physical threats to your dependents.

Examples of Unmet Body Safety Needs:

Example 1: A wife is struggling with an addiction to pain medication. One day, while driving the kids to their after-school activities, she gets into a car accident while under the influence. One of the children gets injured in the accident. This is an example of an unmet need for physical safety in the relationship between the parent and child and also in the marriage.

Example 2: A couple goes out for the evening, and that night, while cuddling, one person initiates sex. When the offer is declined, the initiator pressures the other using phrases like, "You're so selfish" and "You only care about yourself." Without giving verbal consent, the other stops resisting, and just "lets it happen." This is an example of an unmet need for physical safety.

What About Self-Defense?

Self-defense is not an offender to physical safety in a relationship. Self-defense does not equalize responsibility for physical abuse. Self-defense can be an appropriate boundary response to violence.

For example, if your partner, another adult, or a child—of a certain size or strength—comes at you and you close the door to block them, or you kick them as they are hitting you, or you call the cops, or you ask them to leave your shared home, or you restrain them until you can get help, your response is not a physical safety violation; the initial violence is.

If you have a child who is being physically violent with other children, and you restrain them from continuing to hurt the other children until the child can stop being physically violent or until you can separate the children or get help, your restraint or removal of the child to another location is not a safety violation.

If you have any questions about this, please see a professional to determine what type of restraining is appropriate and when.

Physical Safety Category #2: Resource Security

Resource security is another crucial aspect to evaluate when assessing and fulfilling physical safety.

Here, you utilize the following questions: *"Are my essential physical resources safeguarded within this relationship?"* and *"Are there any instances where basic resources are being depleted, withheld, or restricted?"*

During this assessment, you evaluate whether any factors within the relationship, such as conflicts, mood swings, mental health challenges, addictions, choices, or other concerns, threaten your or your dependents' access to basic physical resources in any way.

Examples of violations in the category of resource security:

- Draining essential resources to support compulsive or addictive behaviors, such as gambling, spending money on drugs, alcohol, sex, pornography, etc.
- Making threats to take away basic financial resources.
- Denying access to food, water, or clothing.
- Making threats to or removing access to a shared home without a reasonable plan established.
- Demanding that one receives from a pool of resources, such as time, money, attention, energy, etc., while refusing to help renew.
- Denying access to shared finances or shared bank accounts.
- Making threats or taking actions aimed at limiting the basic resources of dependents.

Examples of Unmet Resource Security Needs:

Example 1: An unmarried couple has been living together. One evening, they engage in a heated verbal argument regarding differing opinions about their social life. The partner who legally owns the home demands that the other person immediately remove their belongings from the shared home and leave that night. This situation represents a violation of physical safety.

Example 2: A woman who relies entirely on her husband's income to support herself and her three children expresses her desire to join the workforce and contribute financially to the family. In response, her husband threatens to revoke her access to their shared bank accounts, stating, "If you don't need me, good luck on your own." This situation constitutes a violation of physical safety.

WHAT ABOUT SEX?

When physical safety is not firmly established, individuals may use sex in the following ways:

- A perpetrator may use sex as a weapon to perpetrate violence, manipulation, or control.
- A victim may use sex to appease their abuser or in an attempt to ensure their physical safety.
- A perpetrator may use sex to appease their victim, creating the illusion that everything is normal and

discouraging the victim from disclosing abuse to others.

- Either the victim or perpetrator may initiate sex in hopes of validating their sense of self-worth or being acceptable despite destructive patterns within the relationship.
- Either the victim or perpetrator may initiate sex to bypass or make up for past negative behavior. In such cases, the term "make-up sex" becomes particularly maladaptive.

PHYSICAL SAFETY VIOLATIONS ARE NOT RELATIONSHIP ISSUES

Sometimes, couples approach Bryce and me seeking guidance on how to address physical safety issues or abuse issues together, as a couple, in a relational way.

While I understand the desire to work things out together, at this level of assessment, I deviate from the approach that "it takes two to tango" and focus on whether or not it is even safe for each individual to engage in the dance.

My view is that while physical safety is a relationship need, physical violence is NOT a relationship "issue." It is a violence issue.

While physical safety violations impact relationships, they are not the responsibility of relationships. I take the approach that the responsibility for assessing and fulfilling physical safety is each person's individual responsibility, and decisions are made unilaterally within the framework of personal responsibility.

That means if you are the victim of abuse or physical safety violations, it is one hundred percent your responsibility to get individual, professional help and to set boundaries that take into account the reality of the situation at hand.

When a victim of physical violence needs support, I prefer to teach them the truth, which is that *they cannot control the other person's decision to be violent or not.* That choice is solely in the hands of the other person and is outside of their control.

Under that reality, if a victim chooses to continue any level of engagement in a relationship where there is past or present abuse, my suggestion is always to get specialized support from professionals for how to assess levels of risk, make decisions about interventions and counseling options, and create safety plans and financial agreements should further violence happen in the future.

Even with the help of professionals and agreements, the perpetrator may choose violence again. Ultimately, they alone make the decision.

If you are the perpetrator in a violent situation, it is one hundred percent your responsibility to get whatever help you need and not engage in physical violence ever again. No one else is responsible for your choice to be violent or act in unsafe ways. You alone are responsible for setting up boundaries that consider your level of individual development and that support you in becoming a safe person in society and engaging in relationships in a physically safe way indefinitely.

Similarly, any action outside of physical violence that ruptures physical safety should be approached in the same way, including active addictions, affairs, etc.

FEELING SAFE VERSUS BEING SAFE

What if there are no explicit physical threats to your safety, but you still feel physically unsafe? This question is an important consideration because the fulfillment of each relationship need encompasses two elements: 1) the fulfillment of that need in reality and 2) your ability to absorb, experience, and receive the need being fulfilled.

An apt analogy for meeting relationship needs is that of meeting the needs for vitamins and minerals. We all require the nutrient iron, and certain foods provide this mineral. However, if you have difficulties absorbing iron, you may consume plenty of iron-rich foods and still show signs of iron deficiency.

If you find yourself in a relationship that is physically safe, but there are instances where you don't feel physically safe due to past trauma, a vivid imagination, mental illness, or other factors, there are resources available to help you bring your thoughts and awareness in line with the present reality. These resources can assist you in grounding yourself and recognizing what is true in the present moment.

I have personally struggled to absorb the reality of physical safety, even in a physically secure environment. Here are some specific examples of situations where I felt fearful despite the absence of physical danger:

- I experienced nervousness that an ex-boyfriend, who had never been physically violent, would break into my house and harm me after he shared something personal with me.
- I felt anxious that a female friend who was actively associating with a spiritual group might become a physical danger to me after I shared with her sensitive information about the group leader.
- I felt afraid that my husband, who had never shown signs of violence toward me, might become violent during a challenging conversation in the early stages of our marriage.

In each of these instances, it is important to note that I was objectively safe. None of these individuals had ever exhibited any signs of physical violence toward me.

In these examples, I was the one struggling to absorb need fulfillment. I was responsible for getting the help or assistance I needed to work through the issue of being unable to absorb the physical safety that was, in reality, there.

Conversely, the opposite situation can also occur. Sometimes, a victim perceives physical safety in a relationship, even amidst physical abuse.

It is not uncommon for abuse victims to dissociate or numb themselves from experiencing pain. In some cases, victims lack the internal or external resources required for their conscious mind to recognize and acknowledge the presence of abuse and lack of safety. I have encountered instances where individuals have asked, "If I don't feel pain during physical abuse, is it still abuse?"

Similarly, in cases of sexual abuse, there are situations where the victim does not experience physical pain, and may even experience physical pleasure despite the context of abuse.

Another scenario pertains to situations where a victim of abuse has never experienced anything different. In such cases, the individual may conclude that they are physically safe within the abusive relationship because it's all they have ever known. They lack a frame of reference for what else is possible.

In clinical and legal settings, abuse is defined by the actions perpetrated, irrespective of whether the victim perceives their experience as painful or identifies it as abuse. The presence or absence of perceived pain or negative sensation does not negate the fact that abuse has occurred. The definition of abuse is rooted in both the actions and their impact rather than the subjective experience of the victim exclusively.

DIFFERENT SHADES OF PHYSICAL SAFETY

Another factor to consider when assessing the fulfillment of physical safety is the gray area—the edges where something goes from safe to unsafe—along with the reality that what fulfills safety for one person may not be what fulfills safety for another.

If you go to an amusement park, you will see that some rides have a ruler at the back of the line. This ruler measures a rider's height and says something like, "Must be 40 inches to ride this ride." In this instance, the same ride that is considered safe for one person may not be considered safe for another.

For physical safety to be fulfilled in a relationship, all individuals involved must both feel safe and be safe. In some instances, it is helpful to delineate the differences in physical safety needs and how potential physical safety violations or resource structures might affect each person uniquely.

For instance, both my husband and I financially contribute to our household. I have a personal need for my husband to have a life insurance policy. In contrast, he does not have that same need to support his sense of physical safety in our relationship. This illustrates how the requirements for physical safety can differ between individuals.

This does NOT mean that it's okay if someone smaller is initiating abuse; it does mean that what it will take for one person to feel safe and be safe may differ from what it will take for another.

Getting an outside, professional opinion when you bump up against the gray area can be helpful in evaluating the situation and clarifying what is needed for each person.

Chapter 4
LEVEL ONE BOUNDARIES

In the realm of physical safety, boundaries support individuals in both creating and maintaining fulfillment of physical safety. The following are examples of boundaries that can be engaged if there are, or have been, any violations or threats to physical safety:

BOUNDARY: Physical Distance, Space, and Separation

This is the first step for most people when there is any imminent physical danger.

Leaving an unsafe situation is a unilateral decision. That means that you can make this decision individually. You do not need to focus on being relational at this moment, and you do not need permission from the abuser to make this choice.

Physical distance initiates the space needed to get safe, assess what's happening, and determine the next steps.

Please note that in some situations, physical separation can escalate violence and increase the risk of harm. An individual can mitigate this risk with the help of law enforcement, professional support, social resources, and the support of family and loved ones.

It may be helpful to remember that physical distance and separation are not meant to be a punishment. The singular goal of these interventions is to establish safety.

If a person threatens harm to themselves or another in response to your leaving or taking space, please remember that you cannot control another person's choice to be violent.

BOUNDARY: Inform Professionals and Begin a Treatment Process

If you are the victim of violence, even if it is a first-time offense, I suggest that you enlist the support of professionals who specialize in helping resolve physical safety issues. With the help of a professional team, you can decide on appropriate next steps.

If you are the one who has initiated physical violence or you are navigating an addiction that presents physical safety concerns, I also suggest that you reach out for professional help immediately. Be honest about what's happened, and be willing to apply yourself to education and support that can help you change your maladaptive responses.

For initiators of domestic violence, there are domestic violence courses, treatment centers, individual therapy, and domestic violence support groups. Your responsibility in all of this is to get help so that you never initiate violence again.

For addiction recovery, there are addiction inpatient and outpatient treatment facilities, as well as addiction therapy and counseling.

Depending on the level of violence or the specific addiction issue and what is being done to address it individually, relationship work may or may not be integrated at some point in the process. I always suggest that victims meet with professionals specialized in issues of violence or addictions to help the victim assess if, when, and how to incorporate relationship counseling or coaching, if ever.

Another thing to know when looking into professional support is that many traditional therapeutic models focus on attending to the feelings of what is called "the wounded inner child."

While this is definitely one part of healing, addressing the feelings of the wounded inner child doesn't necessarily translate into addressing the adaptive behaviors of that wounded inner child, and how those now maladaptive behaviors are impacting relationships.

For example, the ***wounded inner child*** of an abuser may be the aspect of themselves that feels powerless because they themselves were abused as children. The ***maladaptive response*** to that wounded inner child is that when they perceive themselves as powerless, they now abuse someone else.

In this situation, focusing exclusively on the abuser's wounded inner child at the expense of attending to their maladaptive response can harm their current relationships.

This is one reason why victims and all individuals should prioritize boundaries that honor their own safety, even when demonstrating empathy or understanding for those who engage in abusive behavior, harmful addictions, or risky infidelity.

For example, a victim should never be asked to sit in a therapy room and validate the wounded inner child of an abuser, addict, or affair perpetrator prior to receiving sufficient evidence that the impact of the maladaptive response is fully understood, appropriate boundaries are in place, and they are safe. It is also essential that if a victim is being encouraged to hear, understand, or validate another's inner wounded child, they are adequately empowered to acknowledge triggers, take space, and say no to the request.

In the realm of establishing safety, it is so important to find resources that not only focus on individual emotional healing but also on changing maladaptive responses and power imbalance within relationships.

BOUNDARY: Healing for the Victim

Often, individuals who have been victims of abuse, addiction, or affairs feel fear and shame. In response, they may also react from their wounded inner child by exhibiting their own maladaptive behaviors, such as self-harm, retaliation, or silence.

Some examples of these maladaptive responses include ignoring red flags or downplaying minor offenses, hoping things will magically improve.

Another common response is silence, which undermines the foundation for physical safety in relationships with oneself and others.

I know a woman who was the silent victim of domestic violence in her first marriage. When she entered her second marriage, she made a commitment to never stay silent again. This meant that even though her new husband did not exhibit physical abuse, whenever there were any concerns about conflict management, she promptly shared those concerns with professionals, trusted friends, and family members.

Retaliation, or seeking revenge, is another maladaptive behavior that victims may exhibit to soothe themselves or their wounded inner child. While self-defense is an appropriate boundary, retaliation is not. Retaliation is a form of revenge that can perpetuate abusive cycles and hinder a more functional healing process.

If you are a victim of physical safety violations, it is normal to experience difficult feelings and want to respond from your own maladaptive behaviors. For this reason, I encourage you to get the professional support you need to set safety boundaries, heal, and create a beautiful life.

BOUNDARY: Create Protections Around Resources

Combining financial resources and sharing assets is a significant aspect of many marriages, families, and businesses. Establishing well-defined boundaries and agreements around resource allocation can contribute to a solid foundation of clarity and security.

If these agreements were not made or put into writing at the time of joining resources, and especially if there have been threats or attempts to remove or control resources, I suggest getting professional help to create written agreements that lay out the specifics regarding the allocation of resources.

If you depend entirely on someone for your financial support and safety resources, this naturally puts you at greater risk if there is ever conflict.

Not having access to your own resources or the ability to generate them may leave you feeling powerless to stand up for yourself when needed.

If there have been any ruptures in physical safety, this may be a wake-up call to become a financial contributor to your own life or the relationship system. Taking steps to contribute to resource acquisition can empower you and enhance your ability to assert yourself when needed.

BOUNDARY: Create Healthy Boundaries and Support for Dependents

If there have been instances of abuse, neglect, or denial of basic resources to your dependents, it is crucial to seek professional help and establish appropriate boundaries to ensure their safety. This may include the assistance of legal, court, or foster care systems.

This also applies to children who have observed violence in the family or home.

If you are unsure what steps to take, reach out to a therapist, child protective services, or an attorney for professional guidance on how to proceed.

BOUNDARY: Put Safety Plans in Place

In cases where breaches of physical safety have occurred, but sufficient support and effort have been made to genuinely repair and reestablish safety, reconciliation may be an option. If this path is chosen, it is vital to create safety plans that acknowledge the potential for future recurrence.

Working with professionals like counselors, therapists, mediators, and attorneys and having a dedicated support team focused on your safety is crucial for developing a comprehensive plan to define the steps and outline a course of action should another occurrence happen.

FINAL THOUGHTS ON PHYSICAL SAFETY

While not comprehensive, the following list offers a summary of significant themes indicating that the physical safety aspect of a relationship may require attention.

- **You entrust your physical resources** to, or create a dependency on, individuals who have shown themselves to be untrustworthy or who manipulate or exploit your dependence. This could include bosses, parents, spouses, etc.

- **You frequently give** physical resources—such as time, energy, or money—to such a degree that you cannot maintain your own health and self-sufficiency.

- **You engage in habits** that put your body, your money, or other physical resources at risk.

- **You ignore or dismiss** available education that could enhance your ability to experience physical safety with yourself or others.

- **You often make choices** to forgo basic physical safety needs—such as sleeping or eating—for the "benefit" of others.

- **You engage in mind-altering** substances or behaviors that hinder your ability to protect your dependents or adequately meet your own physical needs.

- **You are a healthy and capable adult** without the skills to support yourself financially if needed.

- **You have a child whose behavior** poses physical safety risks to you or other children.

- **You participate** in any level of addiction or compulsive behavior that is physically risky or harmful.

- **You engage** in sexual relationships that may endanger your or another person's physical well-being.

- **You self-harm** or experience thoughts of self-harm that compromise your safety.

- **You struggle** with an eating disorder that impedes your physical safety.

- **You are engaged** in a relationship that involves any form of physical or sexual violence toward you or your dependents.

- **You perpetrate** physical violence or threaten physical resources in a relationship.

If any of these describe you, or your situation, I would suggest making physical safety a priority and getting professional help if needed.

Chapter 5
RELATIONSHIP NEED - LEVEL TWO

The second level of the pyramid illustrates relationship need —Level Two—PSYCHOLOGICAL SAFETY.

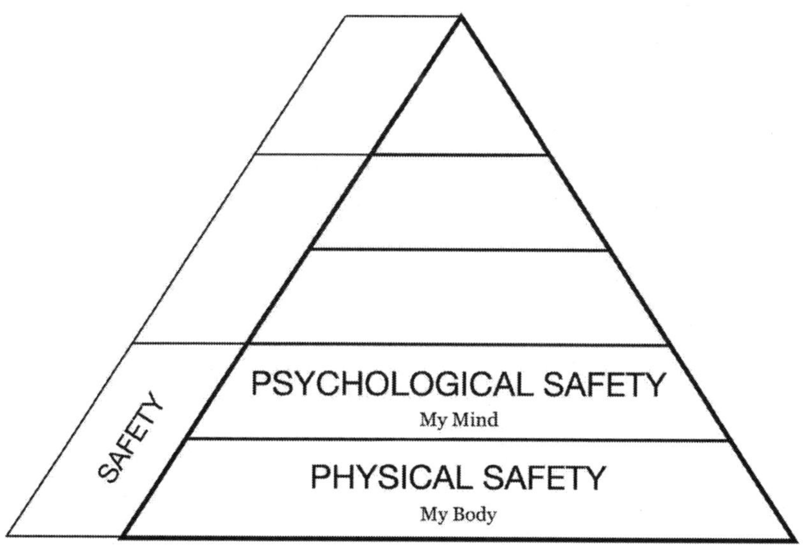

Figure 2 – Hierarchy of Relationship Needs Through Level 2 (Bauer, 2021)

Psychological safety encompasses your mental and emotional well-being within a relationship. Psychological safety violations can be categorized into two main groups: Psychological Abuse and Psychological Neglect.

Psychological abuse – entails emotional, mental, and verbal violence.

Psychological neglect – involves invalidating, ignoring, or disregarding emotional and mental needs.

The subtitle for Psychological Safety is ***My Mind***.

The assessment question at this level is, *"How safe is my mind—my mental and emotional self—in the presence of a specific relationship?"*

This level focuses on the degrees of mental and emotional safety you experience as you relate to your inner world in the presence of a relationship. Psychological safety includes all aspects of your mind, such as thoughts, emotions, beliefs, and the sensations that arise from these aspects.

Similar to physical safety, the fulfillment of psychological safety is the responsibility of each individual unilaterally, as indicated by the *"My"* in the subtitle *My Mind*.

While education and professional support can guide you in assessing and creating psychological safety, ultimately, you alone are responsible for articulating your experiences, drawing final conclusions, and deciding how to proceed with setting boundaries.

Similar to physical abuse—relationship therapy or coaching can be helpful, harmful, or neutral in cases of psychological abuse or neglect, depending on the situation and context.

The risk of harm escalating due to relationship counseling may be highest when the psychological abuse is moderate to severe or the abuser is not committed to taking accountability and changing their behavior.

For this reason, I recommend seeking a professional evaluation from someone knowledgeable in power dynamics and psychological safety to determine if and when to incorporate relationship work into the counseling process when facing psychological safety issues.

WHY ASSESSING PSYCHOLOGICAL SAFETY CAN BE DIFFICULT

Evaluating psychological safety is more complex than evaluating physical safety due to a few primary factors:

- **Assessing psychological impact** is more subjective. We cannot physically observe emotional harm or relational neglect, as they do not leave the clear and visible traces that many physical injuries do. Even when somatic symptoms are potentially linked to a lack of psychological safety, determining the origin of those physical symptoms is not always straightforward.

- **The signals that help assess** psychological safety can vary widely, ranging from blatant actions like yelling and name-calling to more subtle behaviors such as manipulative mind control tactics, discreet eye-rolling, or invisible neglect.

- **It can be difficult to determine** the difference between an action being the root cause of psychological harm or a reaction to psychological harm. For example, is one person's silence a healthy boundary in response to another's criticism, or is someone using silence to punish and manipulate another?

- **The source of psychological harm** may not always correlate with the timing of psychological pain or fear. For example, feeling psychologically unsafe in a current relationship may or may not stem from psychological abuse or neglect in that particular relationship. Sometimes, a person's experience of psychological unsafety is rooted in trauma and safety violations from past relationships.

- **In my experience**, we all, at times, inflict psychological abuse and neglect on ourselves and others. Self-deprecating thoughts such as "I'm such an idiot" can be a form of self-inflicted psychological abuse. Telling a child, "You shouldn't feel mad," can be a form of psychological neglect. Hence, the evaluation of psychological safety is challenged by the reality that we, as a society, are still very much in the midst of a learning curve, working to develop our understanding of psychological safety and how to foster it in more complete and subtle ways.

- **The amount of safety needed** varies according to what level of relationship development someone is working on. What once worked for you may no longer be satisfactory. What one person perceives as sufficient to meet their needs for psychological safety may not be adequate for another.

Despite its complexity, numerous methods exist to consider and evaluate potential challenges to meeting the needs of psychological safety. I will introduce the frameworks I developed and frequently use to assess and determine the meeting of this need. This includes the Model of Masking and the Four Quadrants of Masking.

BACKGROUND ON THE MODEL OF MASKING

I designed the Model of Masking and organized the Four Quadrants of Masking to demonstrate the various ways individuals both initiate and respond to physical and psychological threats in relationships. By examining these responses, you can gather valuable insights that aid in identifying and mapping potential obstacles to establishing levels of psychological safety.

As human beings, we are inherently inclined to be in relationships with others. Various theories propose explanations for why we are so strongly wired for attachment, belonging, and secure connections. Whatever the exact biological reasons, humans are more likely to survive when cared about by others.

Although most of us no longer need to band together for protection against bears, lions, and other tribes, we still rely heavily on each other for access to clean food, strong shelters, medical assistance, and more.

When babies are born, they start observing subtle cues such as body language, tone of voice, and eye movements from parents, siblings, teachers, and peers. These cues alert them to potential danger, including potential abuse or neglect. If a child senses danger, whether real or perceived, they begin to shift their orientation from connection to protection. One of the ways they do this is through masking.

This response to real and perceived threats continues into adulthood. Similar to a child, when an adult senses physical or psychological danger, they often quickly and unconsciously shift into masking.

Masking is a self-preservation strategy employed when it feels unsafe to express oneself authentically. It often occurs unconsciously and automatically as a reactive response. When in a masked state, it is often perceived to be the only feasible choice.

There are two sides of masking: passive and aggressive. The Model of Masking explores these two sides from a one-dimensional viewpoint.

The ***passive side*** of masking encompasses behaviors that retreat from the threat or retreat from the needs of the self, such as pretending, ignoring, denying, hiding, checking out, avoiding, withdrawing, burying, and acting as if everything is fine when it is not.

The ***aggressive side*** of masking includes behaviors that overly engage the threat or exaggerate the needs of the self, such as controlling, coercing, manipulating, blaming, attempting to force change, or pushing fixes for problems you do not understand or that are not in your realm of personal power.

THE FOUR QUADRANTS OF MASKING

The Four Quadrants of Masking is a framework designed to expand your understanding of masking from a one-dimensional to a two-dimensional view.

Understanding masking through this two-dimensional view allows you to comprehend better the complex and multidimensional nature of masking in various contexts. This can help you identify and address these behaviors in yourself and others more effectively.

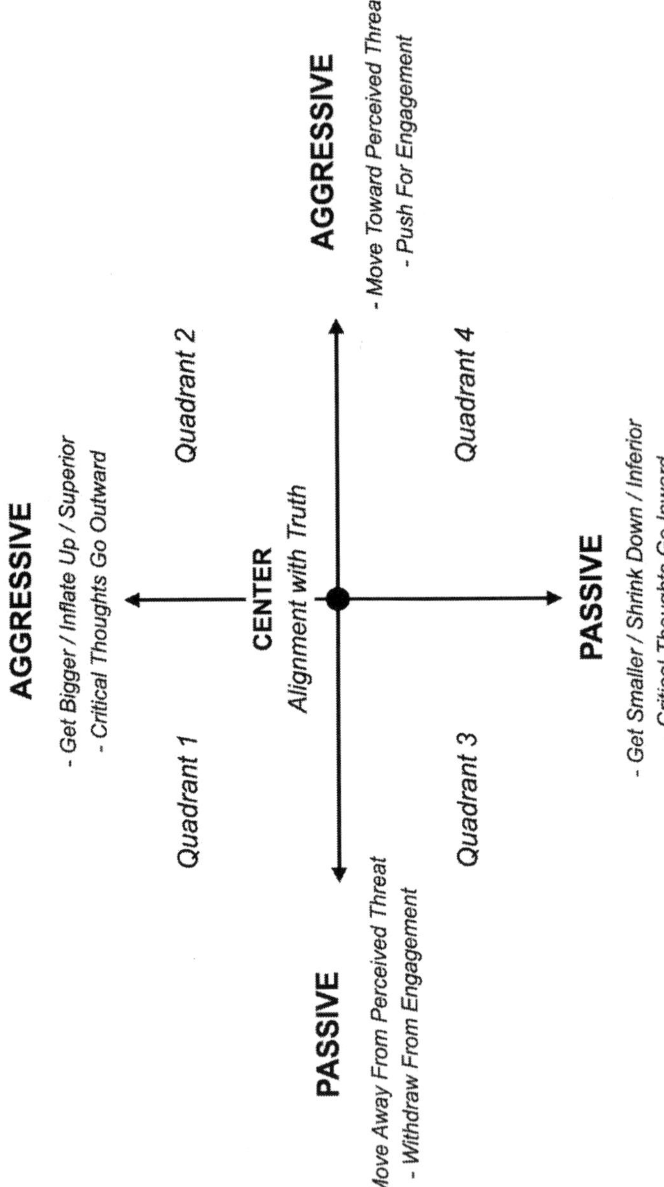

Figure 3 – The Horizontal and Vertical Lines of Masking

Within this four-quadrant paradigm, the vertical and horizontal axes symbolize two different directions of passive and aggressive reactions. The middle, labeled center, represents alignment with your truth, the reality of your inner and outer world.

Center

Drawing upon a yoga analogy, center symbolizes the reality of a pose you desire to embody. As you practice the pose, you may sway left, right, forward, and back as you attempt to create the pose. When you find that moment of alignment where you balance and express the pose as intended, you have reached center. Center is where the truth of your abilities, external reality, aligns with the truth of your desire, internal reality.

In relationship work specifically, center represents the truth of the relationship experiences you want to create. For instance, you might desire the experience of appreciation. The Four Quadrants of Masking symbolize the directions you may sway as you attempt to align yourself with the truth of your desire and what it will take to create the outcomes of that desire.

The Vertical Line

This line represents the vertical level of personal power that an individual assumes in response to the truth of their inner world and the reality of their desires.

Moving upward, away from center, represents the aggressive direction where one adopts an inflated or dominant sense of self. Here, one perceives themselves, or their needs and desires, as larger, more significant, or more grandiose than they actually are. From this stance, they are willing to control themselves or others to meet these perceived needs.

In this state, individuals believe that by raising their self-perception above their own or others' authentic selves, they can more effectively achieve their goals. One mindset is that the best way to fulfill a desire is by dominating someone or something into submission. Another mindset here is that one's needs are beyond the ability of others to help, as those others are below them. From this position, critical thoughts are directed outward.

Moving downward, away from center, depicts the passive direction where one identifies with a sense of self that is smaller or less capable than their own or others' authentic selves. Here, one perceives they are unworthy of, incapable of, or below their own needs and desires or the needs and desires of others.

In this state, individuals believe that diminishing their sense of self or inauthentically submitting to themselves or others will facilitate the acquisition of desires. This happens from a stance of being in an inferior position relative to those desires. The mindset here is that one is unworthy of the desired outcome and must be subservient to those who might help create it. From this position, critical thoughts are directed inward toward the self.

The Horizontal Line

This line represents the horizontal level of personal power an individual assumes in response to the external reality of what will help them create their desire.

Moving away from center and toward a perceived problem represents an aggressive response. It signifies a departure from the truth of one's desire and the authenticity of the self toward engagement with a perceived source of conflict or stress.

In this state, individuals believe that engaging with a threat or perceived threat beyond what's truly relevant to their desire will help them fulfill that desire. This approach can be characterized as anxious, controlling, co-dependent, and pursuant.

Moving away from center to further distance oneself from a perceived threat represents a passive approach. It symbolizes a retreat from the truth of the desired outcome and the authenticity of the self in an attempt to avoid a perceived source of stress or conflict.

In this state, individuals believe that engaging with a threat or perceived threat, even if relevant to fulfilling their desire, will exacerbate the situation and hinder attaining what they want. This approach is characterized by avoidance, emotional distance, and unavailability.

The Four Quadrants

When overlaid, the vertical and horizontal lines create four quadrants corresponding to the four well-known stress responses: fight, flight, freeze, and fawn. Each quadrant is also associated with common nicknames and qualities that describe each category.

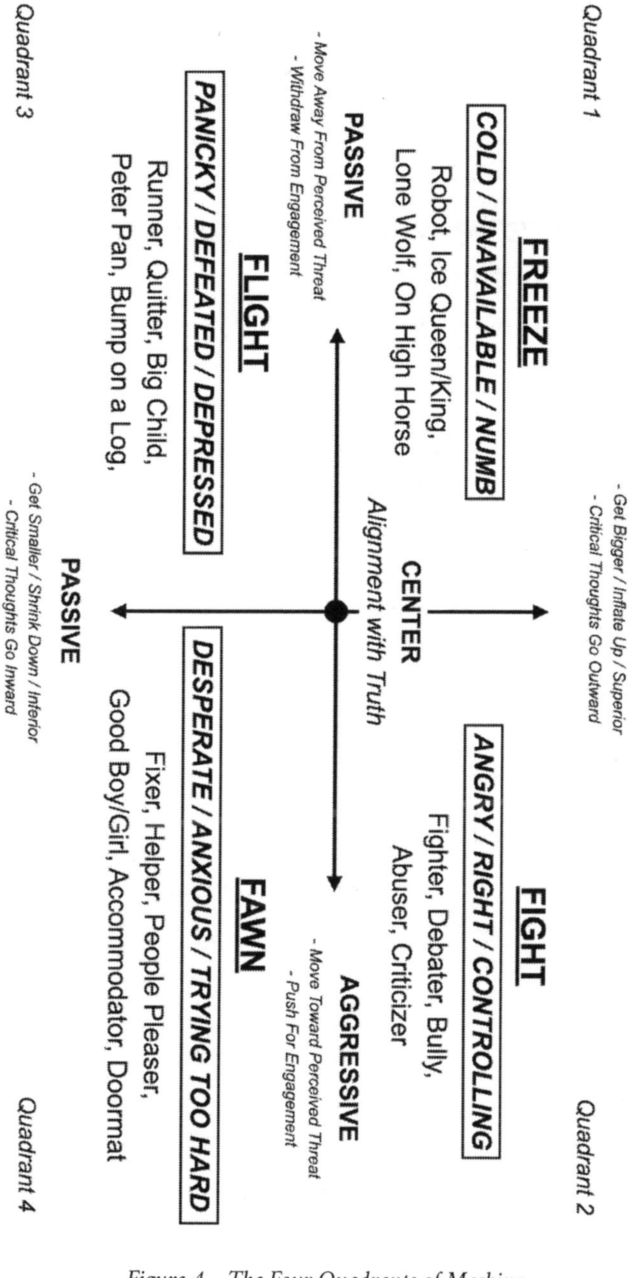

Quadrant 1

AGGRESSIVE
- Get Bigger / Inflate Up / Superior
- Critical Thoughts Go Outward

Quadrant 2

FREEZE
COLD / UNAVAILABLE / NUMB
Robot, Ice Queen/King,
Lone Wolf, On High Horse

FIGHT
ANGRY / RIGHT / CONTROLLING
Fighter, Debater, Bully,
Abuser, Criticizer

PASSIVE
- Move Away From Perceived Threat
- Withdraw From Engagement

CENTER
Alignment with Truth

AGGRESSIVE
- Move Toward Perceived Threat
- Push For Engagement

FLIGHT
PANICKY / DEFEATED / DEPRESSED
Runner, Quitter, Big Child,
Peter Pan, Bump on a Log,

FAWN
DESPERATE / ANXIOUS / TRYING TOO HARD
Fixer, Helper, People Pleaser,
Good Boy/Girl, Accommodator, Doormat

Quadrant 3

PASSIVE
- Get Smaller / Shrink Down / Inferior
- Critical Thoughts Go Inward

Quadrant 4

Figure 4 – The Four Quadrants of Masking

QUADRANT 1: THE FREEZE RESPONSE

Quadrant 1 corresponds to the FREEZE response. This response includes a passive approach on the horizontal line and an aggressive approach on the vertical line. Here, one moves away from center to further distance from the perceived threat or source of conflict while also assuming a position of superiority by inflating one's sense of self above their authentic desire or another.

COMMON NICKNAMES OR DESCRIPTIONS FOR QUADRANT 1 – THE FREEZE RESPONSE

- Ice Queen or Ice King
- Robot
- Too-Cool-for-School
- Lone Wolf
- Too Picky
- On a High Horse
- Unavailable
- Avoidant
- Disconnected
- Distancing

INNER & OUTER EXPRESSIONS OF QUADRANT 1 – THE FREEZE RESPONSE

- Quietly Entitled
- Discreetly Self-Righteous
- Experiencing Disdain

- Experiencing Contempt
- Ignoring Interpersonal Needs
- Considering Others As Inferior or Incapable
- Resistant to Establishing or Relying on Relationships
- Unapproachable or Dismissive due to Perceived Superiority
- Favoring Self-Sufficiency Over Building Trust With Others
- Prioritizing Independence Over Connection
- Unavailable With an Air of Superiority
- Distancing From a Stance of Being Better Than or More Worthy Than Another
- Cold, Harsh, or Uncompassionate

QUADRANT 2: THE FIGHT RESPONSE

Quadrant 2 is associated with the FIGHT response. This response includes an aggressive move on the horizontal line and an aggressive approach on the vertical line. Here, one moves away from center and toward a perceived threat or source of conflict while also moving above one's center to adopt a position of dominance, superiority, or being above one's authentic desire or another.

COMMON NICKNAMES OR DESCRIPTIONS FOR QUADRANT 2 - THE FIGHT RESPONSE

- Fighter
- Bully
- Abuser

- Teaser
- Debater
- Troublemaker
- Dictator
- Tormentor
- Arguer
- Tyrant
- Controller
- Oppressor
- Aggressor

INNER & OUTER EXPRESSIONS OF QUADRANT 2 – THE FIGHT RESPONSE

- Reactive
- Agitated
- Inflamed
- Overtly Self-Righteous
- Openly Critical
- Exerting Control From a Stance of Superiority
- Insistent on Being Right
- Engaging in Emotional, Verbal, or Physical Violence
- Feeling Justified in Abusive Behavior
- Resorting to Blame to Satisfy Needs
- Belligerent
- Quarrelsome
- Employing Logic to Assert Correctness & Maintain Power
- Utilizing Fear or Anger to Maintain Control
- Unaware of the Consequences of One's Actions

QUADRANT 3: THE FLIGHT RESPONSE

Quadrant 3 corresponds to the FLIGHT response. This response includes a passive approach on the horizontal line and a passive move on the vertical line. Here, one moves away from center to further distance from a perceived threat or source of conflict while also moving down from their center, taking on a position of being smaller or weaker than, inferior to, or incapable of aligning with their true self and authentic desires.

COMMON NICKNAMES OR DESCRIPTIONS FOR QUADRANT 3 – THE FLIGHT RESPONSE

- Runner
- Worrywart
- Deer in the Headlights
- Failure to Launch
- Peter Pan Syndrome
- Nervous Nelly
- Big Child
- Handwringer
- Defeatist
- Fatalist
- Bump on a Log
- Lazy
- Anxious
- Hopeless
- Despondent
- Depressed

INNER & OUTER EXPRESSIONS OF QUADRANT 3 – THE FLIGHT RESPONSE

- Frequently Feeling Fear
- Experiencing Despondency, Hopelessness, or Depression
- Preoccupied With Securing an Escape Route
- Sensing Entrapment When Escape Seems Impossible
- Finding Adulthood or Life Overwhelming
- Believing Self to be Inadequate
- Unavailable Due to Perceived Inadequacy
- Distancing From a Stance of Being Unworthy of, Undeserving of, or Less Than.
- Struggling With Self-Trust
- Prone to Panic
- Mired in Shame and Feelings of Insufficiency
- Hesitant to Engage With Another
- Afraid to Acknowledge One's Desires
- Struggling to Fulfill Commitments or Sustain Motivation

QUADRANT 4: THE FAWN RESPONSE

Quadrant 4 is linked to the FAWN response. This response includes an aggressive move on the horizontal line and a passive move on the vertical line. Here, one moves away from center and toward a perceived threat or source of conflict while simultaneously moving down, away from center, taking the position of being smaller or weaker than, inferior to, or incapable of in relation to their true desires or others.

COMMON NICKNAMES OR DESCRIPTIONS FOR QUADRANT 4 – THE FAWN RESPONSE

- Accommodator
- Good Girl or Good Boy
- Mr. Nice Guy or Ms. Nice Gal
- Fixer
- People Pleaser
- Appeaser
- Co-Dependent
- Sidekick
- Helper
- Doormat
- Groupie
- Martyr
- Servant
- Sacrificer
- Bread Crumb Taker
- Ball and Chained

INNER & OUTER EXPRESSIONS OF QUADRANT 4 – THE FAWN RESPONSE

- Constantly Prioritizing Others' Needs Over One's Own
- Feeling Desperate for Validation
- Settling for Breadcrumbs
- Obsession With Idealized Relationships
- Believing One's Authentic Needs Are Excessive
- Frequently Seeking Approval

- Habitually Assuming the Role of Supporter, Cheerleader, or Counselor
- Equating One's Value With the Ability to Help
- Scared to be honest or give productive feedback
- Continuously Smiling, Regardless of Genuine Emotions
- Bearing the Sole Burden of Emotional or Relational Labor
- Concentrating on Being Pleasant or Saying the "Right Things"
- Using Frequent Flattery or Insincere and Excessive Praise
- Believing One Must Always Be Accessible to Others
- Tracking Others' Needs with Hypervigilance

That covers all four quadrants of masking. You can access a full-sized free download of this chart at:

www.jennymorrow.com/bookbonus.

ADVANTAGES AND DISADVANTAGES OF MASKING

Even though the only place from which you can fully express the truth of your desires is center, masking can serve the vital purpose of cuing you into imbalance in a way that helps you learn how to balance.

Masking may also be used as a survival strategy when attempting a relationship "pose" without adequate preparation and before establishing clear and effective boundaries.

At the same time, masking can lead to physical or psychological injury, foster limitation, and block desire. The risk is highest in situations of unconscious masking, identifying with masks, getting stuck in masking, acting out from a mask, and not addressing, balancing, or resolving the needs represented by masking.

In these situations, masking can:

- Become maladaptive—continuing even if there is no threat, or the threat has subsided.
- Support stuckness.
- Cause harm.
- Distort an accurate view of reality.
- Make it difficult for others to see the real you.
- Lead to undesired outcomes or get you into trouble with your relationships, job, the law, etc.
- Remain the primary response to genuine threats despite the availability of more effective solutions.
- Keep you from getting the help you need.
- Lead to coping strategies that, when mild, create unnecessary inconvenience and, when extreme, can severely damage your life and relationships.
- Leave you feeling isolated and alone.

Once you understand the four quadrants of masking, you can utilize the model as a feedback loop to identify perceived threats, adaptive behaviors, and maladaptive behaviors in yourself and others.

STAYING IN HARMFUL CYCLES

I believe some people settle into damaging cycles of masking and psychological harm because they haven't "yet" seen it destroy the relationship.

After years of client work, I have observed that in many of these relationships, there is a point at which something changes. Imagine the metaphor of a bucket filled with water. For some time, the water stays in the bucket, and then suddenly, there is an overflow point, and what didn't seem to be a problem is now making a big mess.

Relationships have similar change points, where what was once tolerable suddenly becomes intolerable.

I have heard more than a few clients tell me they felt blindsided when their spouse "suddenly" wanted to end the marriage.

Prior to reaching Level Four in the hierarchy, individuals rarely seek out relationship education or relationship support of their own volition. In relationships limited to fulfillment of levels one, two, or three, individuals may desire psychological safety, but they rarely see the value of investing in learning or consciously understanding the nuances of psychological safety.

It is common, as individuals and relationships develop, that people become more and more interested in learning about and fostering not only a fulfillment of the obvious layers of psychological safety but the more subtle layers as well.

IMPORTANT QUESTIONS FOR ASSESSMENT

When I use the four quadrants of masking to help clients assess psychological safety, I ask myself, "Is the mask that someone is using":

1. A ***source*** of abuse or neglect in a relationship?
2. A ***response*** to abuse or neglect in a relationship?
3. Part of a normal balancing process?
4. Any combination of the above?

Essentially, masking can signify any of the above. While unraveling the patterns and gauging reality may require patience, understanding the concept of masking offers a pathway to discern psychological power dynamics and evaluate psychological safety.

OTHER MODELS FOR ASSESSING PSYCHOLOGICAL SAFETY

While I often use the model of masking and the four quadrants to assess psychological safety, a variety of other models exist that also aim to assist individuals in articulating their experiences in the area of psychological safety. Below is a list of some of those models.

John Gottman's Four Horsemen of the Apocalypse

John Gottman, a psychologist and world-renowned marriage researcher, lists four communication habits that indicate a lack of psychological safety in a marriage. If not resolved, these habits predict a high chance of divorce (Gottman, 1995).

These four habits include criticism, defensiveness, stonewalling, and contempt. An internet search on "John Gottman's The Four Horsemen of the Apocalypse" will bring up many articles that you can read to educate yourself further.

At the time of this writing, you can learn more about the Four Horsemen here ("The Four Horsemen," n.d.):

https://www.gottman.com/blog/the-four-horsemen-recognizing-criticism-contempt-defensiveness-and-stonewalling/.

Steve Hassan's BITE Model of Authoritarian Control

Steve Hassan formulated the BITE model to delineate the specific tactics and techniques employed by cults to recruit and maintain control over their members (Hassan, 1988).

Familiarizing yourself with this model can provide insight into psychologically harmful methods that may occur not only within groups considered cults but also within families, religions, business relationships, marriages, and so forth.

At the time of this writing, you can learn more about this model here ("BITE Model," n.d.):

https://freedomofmind.com/cult-mind-control/bite-model/.

Attachment Theory and the Attachment Styles Model

Attachment theory and attachment styles provide insights into how individuals respond to interpersonal stress within relationship dynamics. Attachment theory originated from the joint work of John Bowlby (Bowlby, 1969) and Mary Ainsworth (Ainsworth, 1978) and was initially designed to understand parent-child connections.

This theory has since been expanded within the fields of marriage and family studies to include an understanding of adult-adult relationships (Hazan & Shaver, 1987). It offers valuable perspectives on how early attachment experiences shape our relationship blueprints and determine how we, not only as children but also as adults, navigate safety and security in our interactions with others.

What is referred to as *secure attachment* could be likened to the concept of *center* in the four quadrants of masking—with the various insecure attachment styles diverging from secure attachment, as represented by combinations of the different quadrants.

For a more detailed understanding of attachment styles and how they can impact the fulfillment of safety, a simple internet search on attachment styles and relationships will bring up many articles.

Other Leads to Learn More

The topic of psychological safety is quite extensive. There are a variety of search terms that you can input via an internet search to learn more. Some examples of search terms include:

- What are manipulative mind control strategies
- What is emotional abuse?
- What is emotional neglect?
- What are Covert abuse tactics

These phrases will bring up more information if you want to dive deeper into understanding the subtle and not-so-subtle layers of psychological abuse and psychological neglect.

Commitment and Psychological Safety

Nearly two decades ago, I heard a therapist-mentor say: "Whoever cares the least has the most power in a relationship." I don't remember delving into the meaning or intent of their message at the time. However, I have since heard similar expressions from others and have reflected on the idea.

I now believe that while this assertion can *seem accurate,* particularly in relationships that don't progress beyond Level Three, it doesn't genuinely reflect reality. The limitations of this viewpoint become more evident as relationships develop beyond the first three levels of the hierarchy and into levels four and five.

At earlier stages of relationship development, a person might feel safer—even subconsciously—when they opt for a partner who, at least on the outside, exhibits less or more commitment to the relationship than they do.

When someone is still in the process of establishing safety within themselves, it is not uncommon to choose relationships that reflect, on the outside, the imbalance that they are working to resolve on the inside.

Such situations can trigger significant internal and external discord, as differing levels of commitment might feel both more secure and less secure simultaneously.

This approach to commitment will dissipate as relationship development moves up the hierarchy until it will no longer be of interest to invest in relationships with others in imbalanced ways.

THE DIFFERENCE BETWEEN FEELING THAT PSYCHOLOGICAL SAFETY IS MET AND IT ACTUALLY BEING MET IN REALITY

Similar to physical safety, fulfillment of psychological safety includes 1) the fulfillment of safety needs in reality and 2) one's ability to absorb the fulfillment of these needs.

Someone can act in psychologically unsafe ways even when they have no intent to harm. A lack of education, exposure to unskillful modeling, or unconscious choices to dominate or control can leave a person engaging in psychological abuse or neglect while unaware of the harm that they are creating. They may even inaccurately believe that the neglect or abuse they are initiating is in service to the other or the relationship.

A victim of psychological abuse or neglect may be unaware of the neglect or abuse or not perceive it as such. Sometimes, individuals subjected to psychological harm believe that they are the problem and are unworthy or undeserving of psychological safety or care. In some cases, victims have been taught or manipulated into believing that the abuse or neglect is benign or even beneficial for them. They might be told, often by the source of abuse, that the patterns of control and dominance are in place to ensure their safety, facilitate their spiritual growth, or help them become a better person. In such instances, the needs for psychological safety go unmet, even when the victim doesn't perceive the situation as inherently harmful.

Some victims lack internal or external resources, such as self-confidence, education, financial independence, or sufficient support from others to consciously acknowledge the presence of psychological abuse, psychological neglect, or patterns of control.

In some cases, the victim's experience reflects all that they know. Consequently, unaware of alternative possibilities, they may mistakenly conclude that they are psychologically safe within an abusive or neglectful relationship because it aligns with their limited frame of reference.

On the flip side, one can feel psychologically unsafe, even when no one is acting unsafe. An individual can insist that another is psychologically harming them even when the other is not engaging in psychologically harmful actions. In situations like this, the accusation can be the initiator of damage to psychological safety in a relationship.

For this reason, it can be essential to get educated about psychological harm, including how to assess it, the levels of severity, and the difference between safety, abuse, neglect, and someone simply having a difference of opinion, stating a fact, needing space, feeling a feeling, etc.

If you find yourself in a relationship where there is no presence of verbal, emotional, spiritual, or mental abuse or neglect, yet you still feel psychologically unsafe, it might be necessary to get some support for aligning your perception of reality with the actual circumstance. Depending on your situation, this may or may not include trauma work.

Developing the ability to recognize, embrace, and absorb psychological safety when it genuinely exists is an essential part of fulfilling this need.

Chapter 6
LEVEL TWO BOUNDARIES

The following are examples of boundaries aimed at creating and fulfilling psychological safety:

BOUNDARY: Education

Dedicate time, effort, and resources to becoming educated on emotional, mental, spiritual, and verbal abuse and neglect. This includes becoming educated on control tactics and power struggles.

Earlier in this chapter, I provided a list of models that you can use to explore your own experience of psychological safety more deeply, enabling you to differentiate between true respect and controlling or neglectful conduct. Various books, podcasts, online courses, counselors, and coaches can help educate you on the diverse facets of psychological safety.

BOUNDARY: Professional Support

If you notice recurring patterns that raise concerns about potential psychological abuse or neglect within a relationship, or if you have any doubts about the dynamics of your psychological interactions, seek counseling, mentorship, or coaching from a professional who is well-versed in power dynamics and relationships.

Once you have assessed and established that there is sufficient psychological safety within yourself and in your relationship, incorporating relationship counseling or coaching can be highly beneficial. These resources can assist both individuals in learning how to navigate deeper layers of psychological safety and effectively address any ruptures that may arise.

BOUNDARY: Rebalance Power Dynamics

The presence of power imbalance within a relationship significantly increases the risk of psychological abuse and neglect. For instance, if there are expectations within a couple that one person should have greater access to resources such as money, free time, or attention, or if one individual acts as, or is assigned to be, the dominant figure with the final say, it may be advantageous to seek assistance in restructuring the distribution of power. By constructing a more equal power dynamic, you enhance the overall safety within the relationship and create greater potential for further growth and development.

BOUNDARY: Time-Outs

Familiarize yourself with effective time-outs, as they can be an invaluable tool when navigating conflict. There are various time-out methods that you can explore, and a simple internet search, such as "how to take a healthy time-out during an argument," can provide you with ideas for how to structure a beneficial time-out.

If your initial attempts at implementing healthy time-outs are ineffective, or if professional guidance would be beneficial in evaluating the best way to incorporate time-outs into your specific situation, seek counseling or coaching from a trained professional. They can offer personalized support and advice tailored to your needs.

Healthy time-outs are not permanent time-outs. They will always include a plan for timely and constructive re-engagement with a safe space to address the underlying issues.

If it is unsafe for you to take a time-out due to emotional, physical, or verbal escalation from your partner, or if they pursue you in a way that deprives you of the space you need for a time-out, it becomes critical to prioritize your safety and seek professional help to address the situation.

BOUNDARY: Boundaries Concerning Silence or Neglect

If psychological safety issues stem from one or both individuals adopting a predominantly passive approach, it's crucial to interrupt the cycle. You can do this by expressing your desire for connection and collaboration while acknowledging the challenge of initiating difficult discussions.

You might propose seeking support together by saying, "I'm uncertain about how to approach these tough discussions with you, but I genuinely want to be able to have them. Would you be open to seeking support together to help us navigate these conversations effectively?"

If, after clearly speaking your desires, the other person consistently shows reluctance to seek support and there seems to be negligible progress toward their participation in these vital but challenging discussions, it may be necessary to explore alternative boundary options from the available list, including starting with individual counseling or coaching.

BOUNDARY: Resource Reallocation

Reallocating resources may be necessary to restore psychological safety. Here are a few examples:

- In a business partnership where significant ruptures in psychological safety have occurred, one partner might reallocate a portion of their energy, investment, or attention to another venture or project until there is a resolution of the psychological safety issues at hand.
- In a couple relationship, one partner might designate a separate room as their personal space or bedroom. This can serve as a helpful reallocation of space while the psychological safety challenges are thoroughly addressed and resolved.

- In cases where an individual has allowed numerous psychological safety ruptures to perpetuate, they might opt to redirect funds from their entertainment budget to their counseling or therapy budget, encouraging themselves to prioritize their emotional well-being and utilizing resources to learn how to assert their psychological safety needs.

By strategically adjusting resource allocation, individuals can foster a safer environment for themselves and take steps toward healing and growth in the context of psychological safety with others.

BOUNDARY: Separation or Termination of Relationships

In certain situations, the most appropriate boundary to address psychological safety problems is the separation or termination of a relationship.

A separation can create the space needed to initiate the healing process, even supporting the potential to eventually rebuild and reestablish the relationship if mutually desired and feasible.

Alternatively, in some cases, the separation is intended to facilitate a permanent relationship dissolution.

When considering the structure of separations or the termination of a relationship, seeking professional help can be highly beneficial. Professionals can provide guidance and support in determining the best approach to help ensure the psychological well-being of all parties involved.

FINAL THOUGHTS ON PSYCHOLOGICAL SAFETY

Although assessing and establishing psychological safety can be nuanced, subtle, and complex, and our understanding of it is still evolving on a large scale, it is crucial to recognize the significance of psychological safety in relationship development.

As we continue to deepen our understanding of psychological safety and its impact on both physical and mental health, it becomes increasingly important to prioritize its cultivation within our relationships. By fostering an environment of psychological safety, we create a foundation for open communication, emotional well-being, and personal and relational growth, ultimately enhancing the quality and resilience of our relationships.

Chapter 7
RELATIONSHIP NEED - LEVEL THREE

FRIENDSHIP is the third level in the Hierarchy of Relationship Needs.

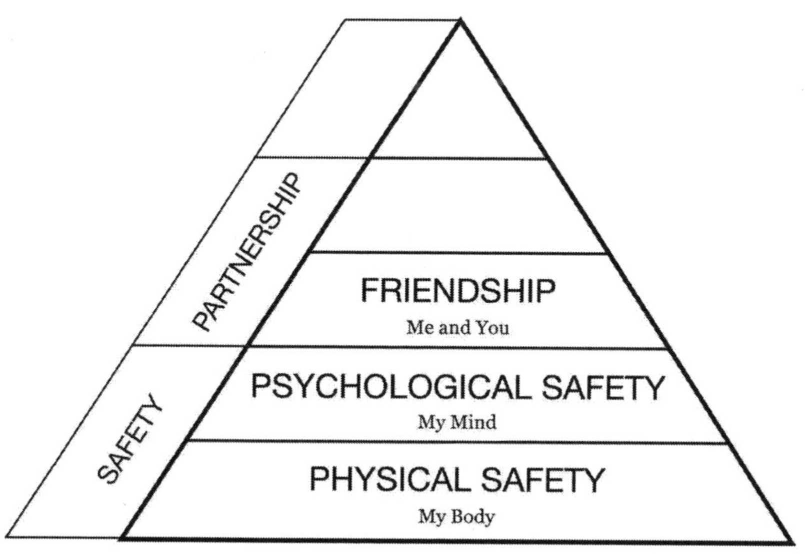

Figure 5 – Hierarchy of Relationship Needs Through Level 3 (Bauer, 2021)

Once safety needs are sufficiently met, FRIENDSHIP needs begin to emerge.

In the context of relationship needs, I define friendship as:

> *The care, love, connection, or liking that you experience for someone with whom there is a sharing of the external world and with whom there is a mutual reliance based on complementary, individual interests.*

The establishment and fulfillment of friendship, as a relationship need, typically entails four essential requirements:

1. A bond or connection related to the external world
2. Time to experience that bond or connection
3. A mutual reliance based on complementary, individual interests
4. Positive association

By exploring each of these requirements, we can better understand the distinctive elements that contribute to the formation of friendship as a relationship need and what type of boundaries will best contribute to the establishment and fulfillment of this need.

A Bond or Connection

Friendship necessitates the presence of bonds or connections between individuals. In friendship, bonds are initiated through having a particular sameness or shared experience that relates to the external world, such as:

Common Interests or Desires – This could include having a common interest in mountain biking, quilting, Indian food, attending music festivals, personal growth and development, etc. These commonalities can ignite interest, care, liking, or love and may lead to further bonds and connections.

Shared Experiences – Shared experiences include growing up together, raising children together, or working together. These shared experiences can foster the initiation of bonds or connections through the experience of camaraderie, creating memories, experiencing the ups and downs of a situation, or a mutual understanding of a shared experience.

Time Spent Together – Examples of time spent together include working together, living together, volunteering together, or sitting next to someone during a three-month college course. Spending time together creates opportunities for shared experiences and conversations that can facilitate bonds and connections.

Belonging to the Same Group – Belonging to the same group can refer to broad categories, such as both being female, Christian, speaking French, or owning dogs, to more specific or localized groups, such as being members of the same neighborhood book club, belonging to the same family, or actively participating in the same kite surfing community. The familiarity and shared identity that can come with belonging to the same group can facilitate the formation of bonds or connections.

Time to Experience the Bond or Connection

After establishing a connection related to the sharing of something in the external world, sufficient time to experience the bond and create new ones must pass for it to evolve from a pleasant connection with a stranger or occasional interactions with a valued acquaintance into the fulfillment of friendship—as a relationship need.

Consider the following examples in which friendship is both initiated and established:

Example 1: At a social gathering, two individuals cross paths and begin discussing their shared passion for books. This initial bond ignites the potential for friendship, and the couple starts going on weekly dates, spends more time together, and eventually gets married. As the years unfold, the fulfillment of their friendship is deepened and strengthened through experiences of many shared activities, such as raising children, buying and selling homes, and creating a shared community. In this particular scenario, the couple describes their relationship as being filled with love and care.

Example 2: Two women meet while attending a local dance class. While dancing beside each other, they laugh over their struggles to master the dance moves. This shared experience becomes a bond between them, and in the following weeks, they continue to stand next to each other in class. After the final session, one woman invites the other out for lunch. They make a habit of meeting regularly, deepening their bond and forming new connections. After approximately two years, one of the women relocates to another state, reducing the frequency of their communication. Nevertheless, the time spent together has fulfilled a meaningful level of friendship for both individuals.

In each of these examples, the initial bond is not only experienced momentarily but is extended over time through multiple experiences that both reinforce the initial bond and create ones.

A Mutual Reliance Based on Complementary, Individual Interests

Friendship begins the orientation into partnership (refer to Figure 5).

Partnership involves an agreement, whether explicit or implicit, in which two or more individuals come together to progress shared interests.

The subtitle for friendship is "***Me and You***," and the orientation of friendship is reciprocity. Here, the shared interests of partnership are complementary, individual interests—"I'll help you if you'll help me." In these situations, both individuals have some level of individual reliance on the other.

Examples of complementary, individual interests include:

Example 1: Two young school friends rely on each other to provide regular recess companionship.

Example 2: A basketball coach depends on having a team to lead, while the team relies on the coach's expertise to become the best they can be.

Example 3: A father relies on his children to embrace his identity as a father, and in turn, his children depend on him for physical and emotional support.

Example 4: Samantha relies on her friend Kate as a sounding board for her daily stress, and Kate relies on Samantha to watch her kids when she needs to run errands.

These examples illustrate how different types of partnerships can exhibit a reciprocal reliance to fulfill individual needs. This aspect of mutual support and interdependence is a significant quality of friendship fulfillment.

Positive Association

Another requirement for friendship is *positive association*. You may have an initial bond, spend time together creating connections, and have a mutual reliance, but if you do not associate positive feelings with the other, and especially if you experience mostly negative feelings, it is unlikely that the need for friendship will be fulfilled.

Marriages that start out with a spark and friendships that begin with a bang can quickly lose their luster if positive association diminishes.

Chapter 8
LEVEL THREE BOUNDARIES

We have now reviewed each of the four requirements for friendship, including a bond or connection, time to experience the bond or connection, mutual reliance, and positive association. When these four qualities come together, you have the establishment and fulfillment of friendship, as defined in the context of the hierarchy of relationship needs.

Next, we will look at the potential challenges to friendship and the boundaries that can support the development and enhancement of friendship.

The concept of boundaries, as viewed through the framework of relationship needs, typically brings to mind the ability to protect oneself from relational harm. This is an accurate portrayal at levels one and two, where boundaries are used to create physical and psychological safety.

However, upon reaching Level Three, the objective of boundaries transitions from ensuring safety to creating and supporting the fulfillment of friendship.

To establish and strengthen the fulfillment of friendship, one can engage boundaries that:

1. Create opportunities to form new bonds and connections related to sameness or shared experiences in the external world.
2. Nurture and appreciate existing bonds.
3. Support mutual reliance in advancing complementary, individual interests.
4. Foster opportunities to generate positive experiences.
5. Mitigate challenges to friendship.

The following are specific examples of boundaries that you can use to support each of these areas of friendship, along with boundaries designed to help you mitigate the challenges of establishing and maintaining friendship.

BOUNDARIES that create opportunities to form new bonds and connections related to the external world.

- **Organize date nights**, excursions, or trips where you share enjoyable activities. This could look like dining out, attending a concert, or visiting a vacation home.

- **Try new things together** such as exploring a new location, trying a new restaurant, or embarking on a new hike.

- **Engage in conversations** about each other's interests and shared interests. These might be conversations about family, community, finances, food, music, or work.

- **Collaborate on projects** such as planning an event, cultivating a garden, writing a book, or completing a home project.

- **Utilize icebreakers** or "get to know you" games.

- **If you want to find** a dating partner or make new friends, attend local meetups, join groups and clubs that align with your interests, and get involved in dating websites or friendship apps.

BOUNDARIES that nurture and appreciate existing bonds

- **Identify common areas of interest** and engage in activities you both enjoy. For instance, if you both love indie rock, attend concerts together. If entrepreneurship is a shared passion, consider taking business courses together or starting a joint venture.

- **Schedule consistent time** to have shared conversations about mutual interests and engage in activities you both enjoy.

- **Acknowledge and express appreciation** and positive affirmations related to the bonds and connections that you've formed, such as, "I love watching you care for our daughter," "It's so fun to eat and enjoy Italian food together, " or "Thank you for always being so on top of the payroll for our business."

BOUNDARIES that foster mutual reliance in advancing complementary, individual interests

- **Use clear communication** to create agreements around complementary, individual interests. For example, say, "I'll pick up the balloons for our son's birthday party if you'll finish frosting the cake." or "I can handle the marketing for our startup if you take charge of customer support."

- **Be mindful of any changes** in implicit or explicit agreements. If circumstances shift, openly acknowledge it. For instance, you could express to your partner, "I've been vacuuming on Saturdays while you mow the lawn, but I'd prefer to do food prep instead. Let's find another solution for vacuuming."

- **Support each other's hobbies** and interests. Suppose your partner loves outdoor activities like hiking in the mountains while you prefer museums. In that case, you can make arrangements to take turns watching the kids, allowing each other to enjoy individual hobbies. Alternatively, consider sharing experiences by getting a babysitter and participating in each other's hobbies together.

BOUNDARIES that foster positive association

The Five Love Languages, presented by Gary Chapman (Chapman, 1995), is a good framework for identifying specific ways to give and receive love at this level of relationship development. Utilizing boundaries based on the five themes can foster positive association.

- **Kindness, validation, affirmation**, caring tones, and words expressing love, admiration, appreciation, and respect, can support positive affections.

- **Dedicated quality time** together, uninterrupted by distractions, frequently enhances positive experiences.

- **Thoughtful gifts** can demonstrate love and care, strengthening connections and nurturing positive feelings.

- **Serving Another** by taking on the work of their chores or tasks often promotes positive association.

- **Physical touch**, such as cuddles, hugs, kisses, sex, or sensual rubs, can highlight positive perceptions.

CHALLENGES TO MAINTAINING THE FULFILLMENT OF FRIENDSHIP

After establishing a friendship, it can be nurtured, maintained, strengthened, or weakened. The following are common challenges that can arise when working to establish and maintain friendship:

1. Established bonds can be challenged, broken, or changed.
2. Resources that were previously used to facilitate bonding might become limited, withdrawn, or redirected.
3. Complementary, individual interests may change or become competitive interests.

4. Positive associations previously established can fade, be forgotten, or be replaced by negative feelings.

Below are some specific examples of what these challenges can look like, along with boundary ideas that can be applied to navigate these challenges.

Challenges to bonds

Many things can change the bonds of friendship. These changes can be perceived as favorable, unfavorable, or neutral. Some examples include:

- A child raised to take over the family business shares that they have chosen another profession.
- The pottery class, where new friends met, comes to an end.
- One partner wants to relocate from a city that both individuals once loved.
- One person departs from the religion that both individuals once followed.
- One person in a friendship chooses to pursue sobriety when alcohol has been central to that friendship.

Challenges regarding resources

Resources previously used to facilitate bonding become constrained, scarce, withdrawn, or reallocated. Here, various factors, such as time, money, attention, and other resources that once enabled bonding, become restricted, limited, withdrawn, or redirected for different reasons. Here are some examples:

- A couple has a baby and struggles to find the consistent, quality time they once had to play tennis together.
- Family funds previously used for a yearly beach trip are now redirected to cover medical expenses following a diagnosis.
- An individual enrolls in graduate school, limiting the time available for hiking with friends.
- A parent's experience of playing games and watching movies with their child on Saturday nights is interrupted as the child grows into their teenage years, choosing to spend more time with friends outside the home.

Challenges to complementary, individual interests

Complementary, individual interests can change or become competitive interests. The following are examples:

- A couple faces a shift when one partner, who chose to stay in the marriage for the children, watches their youngest child leave for college and realizes they no longer rely on their partner for access to daily time with the children.
- A co-founder takes what they have learned from their business partner, the other co-founder, and creates a competitive brand separate from the company they started together.

- Two friends who once exchanged child care support find themselves engaging less and less when one hires a nanny and no longer requires assistance from the other.

Challenges to positive associations

Positive associations, once experienced, can fade, be forgotten, or be replaced with negative feelings. Factors that contribute to this include:

- Experiencing any of the challenges listed above, such as challenges to bonds, resources, or complementary individual interests.
- Ruptures in Level One or Level Two—physical safety or psychological safety.
- Resistance to relationship growth, including the emergence of Level Four.

Boundaries for Navigating Friendship Challenges

Many of the same boundaries that help you create and maintain friendship can also help you navigate and mitigate challenges to friendship. These boundaries were listed earlier in this chapter.

Other boundaries that specifically address friendship challenges include:

- Grieve old bonds and create new ones.
- Explicitly address resource challenges and form new agreements.

- Address any changing individual interests and identify new ways to develop a mutual reliance.
- Acknowledge and address safety ruptures.
- Turn your attention to other friendships or activities if needed.
- Leave or end a friendship if needed.
- Prepare for and engage in the work of addressing Level Four relationship needs.

A NOTE ABOUT FRIENDSHIP

The emergence and fulfillment of each new level of relationship need will transpire in two manners: naturally and via deliberate effort.

Initially, each level emerges organically as new aspirations for the relationship begin to arise without any conscious consideration of relationship design. For instance, once physical safety is established, the desire for psychological safety appears instinctively. Each level then demands work, intention, and effort to achieve fulfillment and mastery.

While fulfilling all relationship needs requires effort, the experience of friendship can at times appear unique as this level may be characterized by a felt sense of non-effort and ease—as if the fulfillment of love and care within the realm of friendship just "happens."

These moments of easy bonding and connection within friendship can be experienced as intense and exhilarating, tranquil and peaceful, or anywhere in between. Here are some examples that illustrate the ease with which friendship can both emerge and be experienced:

Example 1: Early in a relationship, there can be an effortless sense of bonding, known as the honeymoon period. During this time, connection may feel effortless, enhanced by the excitement of novelty and newness.

Example 2: Certain relationships exhibit an inherent ease of bonding due to shared interests and complementary qualities. For instance, a teenage son who plays baseball may experience an easy bond with a parent who enjoys watching the sport and supporting their child's passion.

Example 3: In some relationships, the passage of time contributes to a deep sense of ease in the bonding. Imagine a contented couple sitting on their porch swing as they observe their children and grandchildren play. In this scenario, they may experience a natural bond related to years of shared experiences.

These examples highlight how the experience of friendship can arise and be perceived as effortless during different stages and phases of relationships.

Because the resting place of friendship can feel so good, many people stop here, imagining friendship as the highest form of relationship development. This is especially true when friendship is blended with the chemicals of novelty, such as in a new relationship, or on the flip side, when friendship is imbued with years of history and comfort together. In these situations, friendship can appear to be a higher level of relationship development than it is.

Considering friendship as a satisfying apex of one's relationship development is not inherently problematic, and many people will find it sufficient. However, clinging to the belief that friendship is the pinnacle of relationship development *so that one can avoid further growth and learning*, especially when Level Four initiators emerge, can lead to suffering.

While friendship requires a certain level of safety to emerge, it is still fundamentally oriented toward survival, where it maintains masking as a potential strategy for building connections and navigating conflict.

To move into the realm of advanced relationships, where there is a fundamental shift in orientation from surviving to thriving, you must be able to develop beyond Level Three and into Level Four relationship needs.

Embracing the idea that friendship is an intrinsically meaningful part of the relationship journey and simultaneously a door to further relationship development prepares you to begin engaging in levels four and five.

Chapter 9
RELATIONSHIP NEED - LEVEL FOUR

When the first three foundational needs are sufficiently met, Level Four—INTIMACY begins emerging.

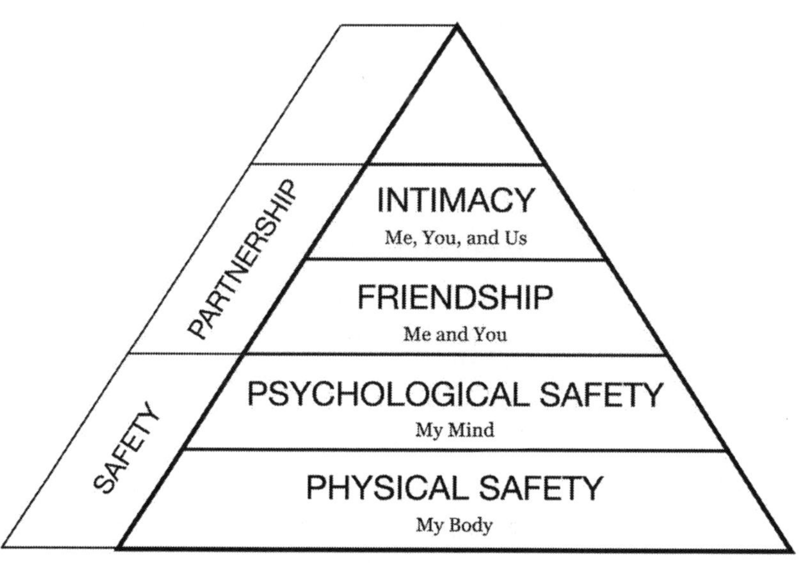

Figure 6 – Hierarchy of Relationship Needs Through Level 4 (Bauer, 2021)

Intimacy has multiple definitions. My definition of intimacy is:

An active engagement with the truth, both internal and external, for the purpose of deeply knowing and experiencing the authentic ME, YOU, and the US.

I have observed, both in myself and others, a longing for something that often proves elusive within relationships. This intangible essence, often challenging to articulate, is the desire for intimacy, and its yearning frequently echoes throughout poetry, music, and art.

While intimacy includes the foundation of friendship, it also transcends it, giving rise to a new dimension of relating that extends beyond the bounds of friendship alone. In intimacy, the bonds of friendship serve as the doorways through which partners can share the truths of the internal realm. Together, you can travel into unseen interior places. These once unexplored spaces house hidden treasures of truth, and the outcome of intimacy is a deeper and broader knowing of reality, an internal waking up.

While friendship emphasizes cultivating connection through shared external experiences and highlights positive feelings, thoughts, and perspectives, intimacy broadens the scope to encompass all things, including the internal and external worlds, differences and similarities, and positives and negatives. Intimacy is the space where all thoughts, feelings, sensations, and behaviors are observed and explored, whether they are perceived as positive or not.

This doesn't imply that inappropriate behavior is tolerated or that safety isn't crucial—recall the hierarchy. For intimacy to truly develop, a solid groundwork of physical safety, psychological safety, and friendship must already be in place.

What it does mean is that in the realm of intimacy, there is a commitment to engaging with the truth and aligning with reality in all of its forms. Developing intimacy employs an approach of observation, acceptance, examination, and action continually arising from deeper and deeper levels of knowing.

Because relational intimacy, including a sharing of the inner world, is generally not taught or nurtured in conventional education, traditional family models, popular careers, or orthodox religious practices, when one is ready for it, it almost always requires additional learning and support beyond these conventional frameworks.

INTIMACY EXPANDS TO INCLUDE ME, YOU, AND US

When assessing and creating boundaries that support Levels One and Two, physical and psychological safety, the scope of assessment and decision-making is on ME.

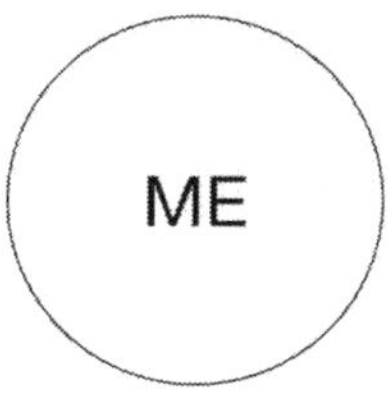

Figure 7 – Orientation of Physical and Psychological Safety

Here, you assess your safety using questions such as:

- How safe is my body in the presence of this relationship?
- How safe is my mind in the presence of this relationship?

You then determine, with professional support if needed, what boundaries are required to create the level of safety that you desire. This may include making changes if you are in an unsafe relationship or environment. It may also include working on your perception of safety if you are, in fact, according to all assessments of reality, safe. At these first two levels, focusing on oneself, the ME is both appropriate and essential.

At Level Three—FRIENDSHIP—the scope of assessment and decision-making widens to include two or more individuals represented by ME and YOU.

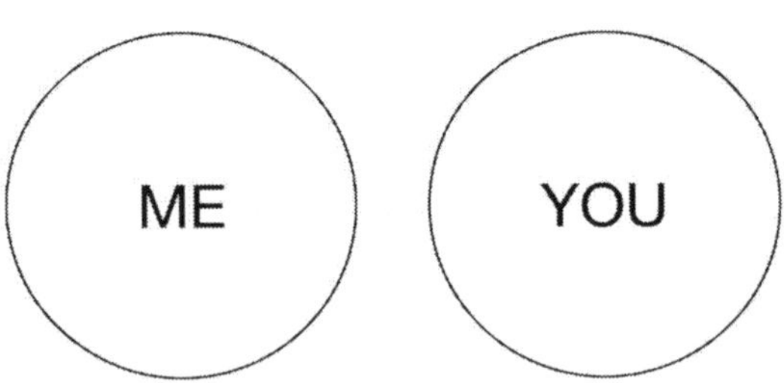

Figure 8 – The Orientation of Friendship

The fulfillment of friendship is experienced through a sense of care, love, or genuine liking for another person. Connections at this level are made through sharing aspects of the external world and identifying opportunities to mutually rely on one another for the progression of complementary, individual interests. At this level, individuals assess their own experience of friendship.

Upon reaching Level Four—INTIMACY—the scope of assessment, insight, and decision-making expands, moving from two positions of awareness, ME and YOU, to three positions of awareness: ME, YOU, and US.

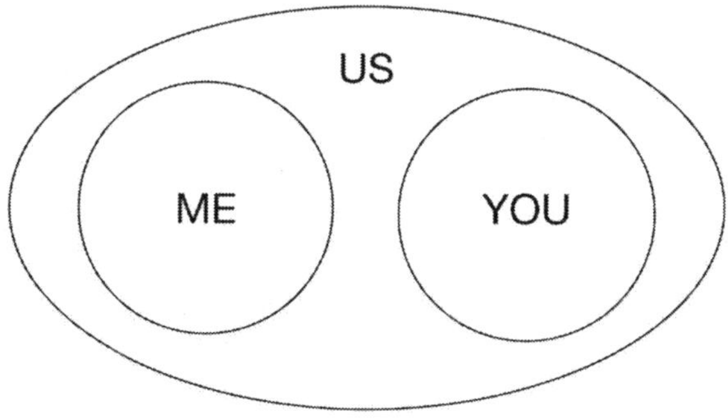

Figure 9 – The Orientation of Intimacy

Intimacy development opens up opportunities to see various facets of reality that can only be accessed through the internal and external of all three viewpoints.

During this phase of the relationship journey, both individual and relational empowerment is enhanced by engaging with more information, moving the entire system toward a greater understanding of the truth.

Here, conflicts, friction, and the convergence of differing opinions and perspectives are not seen as threats, as they might be during friendship, but rather as opportunities for growth. Through this process, individuals learn more about themselves, each other, and reality.

In the realm of intimacy, the primary objective is not actively seeking or cultivating a bond. Instead, intimacy, as illustrated in the hierarchy, is built upon a foundation that includes friendship, where bonds have already been formed and inherently exist.

From this foundation, the focus of intimacy is to utilize preexisting bonds and connections to delve deeper into exploration and access more layers of truth. Subsequently, this heightened awareness of reality fosters a more complete collaboration, enriching the creative process within the collective US or WE.

This expanded collective is aware of things beyond the knowledge of each individual alone and possesses capabilities neither can achieve independently.

DEVELOPMENT AND FULFILLMENT OF INTIMACY

The cultivation of intimacy includes five specific attributes: *attention, equality, curiosity, vulnerability, and courage.*

Attention

Attention is one of your most powerful resources for developing intimacy. It becomes imperative to learn how to employ attention deliberately and consciously, honing the ability to direct and align it in relation to your priority values.

In the context of intimacy, attention refers to your ability to notice, acknowledge, stay present to, and be with the truth of what's happening moment to moment—both internally (inside yourself) and externally (outside yourself).

Equality

Equality refers to balancing relational polarities and eliminating power imbalance between individuals. In the realm of intimacy, dismantling any layers of power imbalance will facilitate the emergence of a more complete truth.

This complex undertaking does not mean disregarding or dismissing roles, responsibilities, or resource disparities. Rather, it involves consciously recognizing, considering, and accounting for these differences.

In various relationships, inherent differentials exist, including role differences—such as those between parent and child, student and teacher, boss and employee, doctor and patient—and those relationships in which there are disparities of wealth, information, time, experience, energy, etc.

To establish fundamental equality despite inherent differences, specific agreements, boundaries, and the support of third parties may be necessary. Without conscious acknowledgment of these differentials, power dynamics can obstruct intimacy and hinder engagement with the truth.

Although marriage partners in the United States are legally recognized as equals, many partnerships still assume traditional mindsets that reflect the lingering stories of inequality from the not-too-distant past. These mindsets, both subtle and overt, continue to shape the dynamics of relationships and, if not explored consciously, can block the very intimacy that so many people long to experience.

Prior to the integration of intimacy, the lower three levels of the hierarchy are willing to tolerate power imbalance to ensure the survival and maintenance of specific external relationship experiences and forms. This is why friendship can take shape amidst fundamental aspects of inequality. For example, a relationship limited to friendship may form even if one person is consistently the main character and the other the sidekick.

Intimacy, on the other hand, requires an awareness of the inherent inner equality that already exists. In the realm of intimacy, each person is equally valid, equally worthy, equally considered, and equally acknowledged.

Curiosity

Curiosity assumes a crucial role in developing intimacy, of which the core intention is to foster engagement with the truth. When individuals approach their relationships with genuine curiosity, it opens the door to exploring deeper levels of reality, which, in turn, promotes the experience of growth and provides opportunities for intimacy. This inquisitiveness sparks a willingness to ask probing questions, actively listen, and be receptive to the responses received.

If physical safety and psychological safety are not well established, curiosity can be dangerous. I have seen victims of abuse who believe that they need to be more curious about their partner, hoping that the intention of curiosity and the development of a more intimate bond will stop the abuse. Please remember that intimacy must be built on a foundation of safety that is already established. Equality, as discussed above, further lays the groundwork for safety at this level.

Vulnerability

As you embrace your own and others' authentic selves, more aspects of your true identity emerge. This unveiling of additional aspects of the self, including parts that were once hidden or dismissed, creates an experience of vulnerability.

The word vulnerability originates from a Latin word that translates as "wound." Vulnerability is the quality of being exposed to the potential for wounding. While this may sound like an undesirable experience—and in dangerous situations, it is—it is also an essential experience for growth and new life.

Imagine a large Sequoia tree whose seeds are tiny. If you were lucky enough to get a Sequoia seed to germinate, it would become a small sapling. Even though the sapling may grow into one of the largest and most indestructible trees in the world, it begins its life as a small and fragile plant, susceptible to the tiniest of threats.

This concept illustrates the internal struggle that numerous individuals encounter when faced with vulnerability or even when witnessing others' vulnerability.

Vulnerability possesses the duality of being both powerful and weak simultaneously. It embodies a newfound vitality and fragility all at once. This inherent paradox can evoke a sense of overwhelm and intensity.

Vulnerability frequently emerges after the dissolution of something that was previously a "limiter." In the example of a Sequoia sapling, this "limiter" would equate to the seed. In the context of relational vulnerability, this limiter often references a limiting belief.

Deconstructing previous limiters or beliefs can feel risky and unnerving, as they may have once functioned as a protective mechanism. For this reason, vulnerability, a necessary stage in the process of relational evolution, is frequently experienced as weak, unstable, defenseless, susceptible, and fragile.

When you can see the paradox for what it is and be with the experience of vulnerability, not backing away from the emergence of new truths about yourself, life, and others, it can reconnect you to your personal and relational power, lighting up the experience of new life and aliveness.

Courage

Even though safety serves as a prerequisite for intimacy, courage still stands as a defining attribute of intimacy development. This is due to the inevitable experience of vulnerability that follows the revealing of new layers of the self.

Even when the foundational three levels are mature enough to allow intimacy to surface, this doesn't mean that achieving intimacy is effortless. Frequently, I notice that when someone is ready to approach intimacy, it can, at first, seem unfamiliar, disorienting, unnerving, daunting, and confusing.

Think of a weight loss reality show. Here, contestants are carefully assessed by physicians before and during their weight loss journey. Despite these safety precautions, embarking on a process that fundamentally transforms one's body and mind can be physically, emotionally, and mentally challenging. Contestants often report that it requires a tremendous amount of courage to confront the daunting and intense nature of such a drastic change and stay committed to the process.

A similar type of courage is essential for fulfilling intimacy, as the journey will unearth profound new truths that stretch each person beyond the edges of their comfort zones. This process demands a willingness to confront vulnerability, become aware of inherent equality, navigate complexity, ask for help, and face the unknown.

INTIMACY REQUIRES CONSENT

Because intimacy is intrinsically linked with attention, equality, curiosity, vulnerability, and courage, it inherently requires consent. This need for consent applies to all dimensions of intimacy, including physical, emotional, mental, and spiritual intimacy.

Within the realm of intimacy, gaining entry into another's inner world in a genuine way can only transpire when such access is truly granted.

Regarding consent, all parties hold equal self-agency when determining the extent of intimacy they want to initiate or engage in. Just because one person desires intimacy does not mean that the other needs to say yes or participate in it, and whether or not someone decides to consent has nothing to do with another's right to request intimacy as an option.

DOES INTIMACY MEAN SEX?

While many people use the word intimacy to refer to sex, sexuality, or physical connection, when looking through the lens of the hierarchy, intimacy is not synonymous with sex. Instead, intimacy refers to a particular way of relating that includes attending to specific relationship needs and a corresponding level of relationship development.

Sex can happen at any level of relationship development—including all three levels prior to intimacy—and can be used in ways that either break down relationship needs, maintain them, or support their fulfillment.

Many intimate connections do not include sexual bonding of any type. For example, you can experience emotional intimacy with friends and family members, intellectual intimacy with a research partner, and spiritual intimacy with a meditation group. These intimate connections can occur without engaging in any physical or sexual connection.

In summary, intimacy is not sex, and sex can occur with or without the presence of intimacy.

Chapter 10
LEVEL FOUR BOUNDARIES

The first two levels of the hierarchy primarily revolve around survival. The third level, friendship, while still oriented to survival, has enough safety established to act as both a resting place and a bridge leading to something beyond survival alone. Level Four, intimacy, marks the first level where the focus shifts toward thriving.

Like establishing boundaries at Level Three, intimacy boundaries are not primarily about safety or preventing negative outcomes. Instead, intimacy boundaries serve the purpose of deepening authenticity and alignment within a relationship.

Nearly two decades ago, I began my work as a Marriage Therapist. People were coming to see me for a variety of reasons, including depression, anxiety, addictions, relationship struggles, and more.

I wondered, “How do I help all of these people?” At the time, many of them were older, more educated, and had more life experience than I did. “What can I give these clients that they don’t already have or know,” I questioned.

It was then that I began to get more curious about what clients really wanted. I realized that whatever the presenting problem was, they were in my office for a specific reason. There was something they desired.

And so I began to ask:

- “What would be different if you woke up tomorrow and your depression was magically gone?”
- “What would be different if you and your spouse could work through disagreements with ease?”
- “What would be different if you no longer struggled with overeating?”
- “What would be different if you were offered the career of your dreams?”
- “What would be different if your biggest stressors, struggles, and problems were suddenly and completely resolved?”

Regardless of the presenting problem, clients shared a variety of aspirations, and their responses to what would be different exhibited similar themes. I frequently heard the following answers:

- I’d feel more relaxed
- I’d be present with my kids

- I'd be motivated to wake up in the morning
- I'd feel like I was living my purpose
- I'd be secure and happy in my marriage
- I'd feel joy
- I'd be healthy
- I'd trust my body
- I'd feel free

I would then go a little deeper, "And then what? What would be different if you felt more relaxed and at peace?"

I continued this line of questioning until clients began to *feel* the experience of what they really wanted.

It seemed that ultimately, deep down, underneath all of the expressions of desire, was a primary core desire.

After years of doing this work, I now believe that that core desire is:

> *To be connected with the truth of who you really are and to remember that who you are is synonymous with the truth of your desires. In this place, your true desires are not separate from you but rather a reflection of you.*

A few years into my work, I learned of Joseph Campbell. Joseph Campbell was a mythologist who spent 50 years studying mythology, cultures, and religions, giving voice to the concept he called *the hero's journey.*

Near the end of his life, Joseph Campbell was interviewed by a man named Bill Moyers, who asked, "You've spent half a century studying humanity. What is it we all really want? Is it meaning? Is that what we want?" (Moyers & Campbell, 1988).

Joseph Campbell responded,

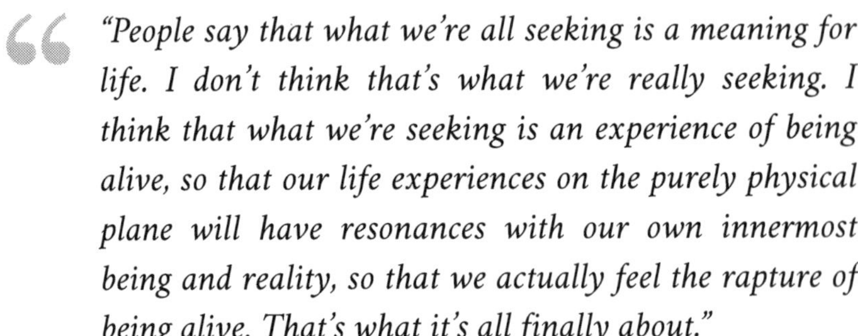

> *"People say that what we're all seeking is a meaning for life. I don't think that's what we're really seeking. I think that what we're seeking is an experience of being alive, so that our life experiences on the purely physical plane will have resonances with our own innermost being and reality, so that we actually feel the rapture of being alive. That's what it's all finally about."*

It seems to me that this is the great benefit of being connected to the truth of who you really are.

This experience of being alive stands as the ultimate reward for the hero's journey into a more authentic life. By embracing your genuine self and aligning with your innermost essence, you step into an honest experience with life and truly live. This is the gift of intimacy.

For this reason, boundaries at the level of intimacy do one thing—they facilitate aligning with and living out of the authentic self.

There are three angles from which intimacy boundaries are established—me, you, and us.

ME: *My intimacy boundaries are for me, about me. They are a conscious choice that I make to create a container in which I can show up as my authentic self.*

YOU: *Your intimacy boundaries are for you, about you. They are a conscious choice that you make to create a container in which you can show up as your authentic self.*

US: *Our intimacy boundaries are for us, about us. They are a conscious choice that we make together to create a container in which our relationship can show up as its authentic self.*

DO OTHERS NEED TO JOIN ME, OR CAN I DO THE WORK OF INTIMACY ALONE?

A common question from potential clients is: "Can I work on intimacy development alone, or do I need another to participate?" This question highlights an important distinction between individual intimacy development and partner intimacy development.

To address this question, I'll use a metaphor. Imagine figure skaters. A solo figure skater learns to skate independently, refining their connection to their body and movements in ways that most people never do. Individual figure skating possesses such depth of possibility that one could spend an entire lifetime progressing their individual figure skating skills.

However, if their aspiration is partner figure skating, they must develop themselves individually, and they must find a partner who can skate or is willing to learn. Partner skating demands that both individuals not only skate proficiently on their own but also learn joint maneuvers that are unattainable to solo skaters.

When a client sees me for individual coaching, I explain that in our sessions, we are working on how they relate to themselves and how they relate to their perception of others. In the realm of self-relationship, the "me" and the "you" of intimacy represent the diverse facets, or parts, of one's self.

Through self-awareness, you cultivate a knowledge of numerous internal parts and their intricate relationships with each other. The concept of "Us" within a self-relationship signifies combinations of these various internal aspects, ultimately culminating in forming a complete self, a whole entity that transcends the influence of any individual part in isolation. Individual intimacy work, by nature of its process, cannot help but impact partner relationship work. Nevertheless, partner intimacy work takes both people.

When a client wants to develop intimacy in partnership with another, we are now combining individual intimacy work and partner intimacy work. Here, self-awareness and awareness of the other dance together, weaving in and out, exploring and expressing each person along with the relationship between the two.

Intimacy work in partnership requires consent, effort, practice, and engagement from both parties. As much as you might hope that you can pick up the slack and do all the work of partnership intimacy on your own, you cannot; it is not even possible.

RESISTANCE TO INTIMACY CAN HALT OR BREAK DOWN RELATIONSHIP GROWTH

The demands of intimacy contribute a weight to the hierarchy. This isn't a problem, considering the substantial rewards associated with intimacy fulfillment. However, it can be an issue if the foundational three levels are not strong enough to hold the extra weight.

Often, clients seek guidance at the level of intimacy because they are ready to grow beyond the limitations of their current level of relationship fulfillment. While guidance can be indispensable for intimacy development, it may be the case that only one person in a partnership is ready to begin the process.

When one individual in a relationship desires intimacy and the other displays hesitation, resistance, or opposition, the resulting imbalance can lead the desiring partner to:

- Persist in their desire for relational growth while continuously facing letdowns.

- Abandon their wish for intimacy development and settle for a relationship experience that falls short of intimacy fulfillment.

- Forgo their longing for intimacy development with a particular person and instead invest in other relationships that appear to, or do, offer opportunities for intimacy development.

- Prioritize their desire to experience intimacy with someone in the role of that particular person, such as a primary partner or spouse. In such instances, the one who desires intimacy may begin to release attachment to the current relationship and initiate the grieving process. As time progresses, it becomes increasingly probable that the relationship's structure will be altered (such as ending a marriage) to make space for new possibilities or, at the very least, attain personal peace.

When any of these scenarios unfold, advancement toward establishing relational intimacy in tandem with that particular other slows down or stops. When this happens, the once-positive associations of friendship may morph into feelings of resentment, pain, anger, and confusion.

Whether in relationship with yourself or another, initiation into intimacy development can feel daunting. For this reason, it becomes crucial to face cues of intimacy initiation head-on and get support when needed.

CHALLENGES TO INTIMACY DEVELOPMENT

There are a variety of challenges and obstacles that can inhibit intimacy development generally. These include:

- **A lack of education**, modeling, or resources designed to support intimacy fulfillment.

- **A deficiency of time or attention**. Many people fill their lives with so many tasks or distractions that there is little time or attention to sit in silence or settle into deeper, reflective observation—with themselves or others.

- **The absence of consent** from one or more parties. Pushing intimacy without consent can break down safety and halt intimacy development.

- **Attempting intimacy** in a relationship that is not prepared for that level of relationship development or not getting the support needed to fortify Levels One, Two, or Three.

- **Believing friendship is the peak** of relationship development or partnership. This belief can lead to resisting differences, hiding negative emotions, or avoiding conflict. It can also lead to the idea that compromise, a form of relationship resolution, is the best way to resolve disputes and differences. While compromise can serve Level Three, friendship needs, it is not the most effective approach for meeting Level Four—intimacy needs.

- **Lack of coaching**. Just as individuals who advance in the ranks of athletics benefit highly from credible coaching and mentorship, so do those who advance in relationship development benefit from coaches, counselors, and mentors trained to facilitate relational growth at Level Four and beyond.

- **Attachment to relationship fantasies**. Many people are conditioned to maintain power imbalance in relationships. If this has been your experience, you may believe that it is your duty, safer, or that it is more fun or romantic to surrender your personal power to another. On the flip side, you may believe that the best way to maintain personal power is to assert control over or be willing to take another's personal power from them. While the first three levels of relationship needs can be met, even amidst power imbalance and inequality, the fourth and fifth level needs, including intimacy, necessitate eradicating power imbalance, including those maintained by relationship fantasies.

- **No access to an intimacy development model**. To master the more intricate aspects of intimacy, a model for regular practice is essential. Just as you must have a model of movement—such as tennis, swimming, yoga, basketball, or martial arts—and consistent practice in that model to master the more advanced expressions of movement, you must have a model of intimate relating that you can practice to master the more advanced relational expressions of intimacy. In this book, you will be learning an intimacy development model that I named the POET Process.

- **There are a variety of fears** that, if left unattended, can pose significant obstacles to intimacy. These fears are generally unconscious and include the following themes:

  - It's not safe to experience intimacy.
  - If I step into intimacy, I will lose myself.
  - There are too many costs to intimacy and not enough benefits.
  - People will take advantage of me if I am open to intimacy.
  - I will be seen as weird, strange, or judged if I initiate intimacy.
  - Intimacy is boring, dull, and lacking in excitement.

- I will have to give up what I really care about if I decide to develop intimacy.
- Intimacy is for another type of person, not for me.
- The changes intimacy might require could threaten my current relationships.
- Intimacy isn't possible. It's just a fantasy.
- If I engage intimacy, I will lose control.

BOUNDARIES FOR CULTIVATING INTIMACY

Boundaries formed to support the progression of intimacy development are crafted to facilitate aligning with and living out of the authentic self and authentic relationships. The following boundaries are antidotes to many of the intimacy challenges listed above.

In addition to these overarching boundaries, we will subsequently delve into more specific boundaries that contribute to each of the five attributes of intimacy.

- **Ensure that the foundational relationship needs** of Levels One, Two, and Three—safety and friendship—are frequently assessed and maintained.

- **Get consent from all parties** who want to engage in intimacy.

- **Get support to process the fears** that might be keeping you from intimacy.

- **Seek third-party assistance** as needed—including mentors, coaches, therapists, books, educational offerings, or courses.

- **Similar to exercise, take breaks when needed**, and if it seems like intimacy work is creating damage, stop and get an assessment of what is happening.

- **Become educated in a process** that can assist you, or you and another, in practicing and strengthening your abilities to engage in the various facets of intimacy. In this book, you will learn the POET Process.

BOUNDARIES TO STRENGTHEN THE FIVE ATTRIBUTES OF INTIMACY

In conjunction with the general boundaries listed above, intimacy development can benefit from implementing boundaries designed to shore up and fortify each of the five individual attributes—the collective effort of which contributes to greater and greater levels of intimacy fulfillment.

You can engage these boundaries individually to deepen self-intimacy or with another to foster intimacy in a relationship.

BOUNDARIES THAT SUPPORT ATTENTION:

- **Establish a meditation** or mindfulness practice.

- **Clearly define and prioritize** your values, consciously deciding where to direct your attention.

- **Eliminate distractions** and create structures and routines that support you in aligning your attention with the priority values.

- **Engage in journaling** practices that enhance your ability to engage with the truth and focus on what matters most.

- **Seek coaching and mentorship** designed to support you in orienting your attention.

- **Foster healthy habits** around sleep, nutrition, exercise, and relaxation. Doing so will support you in your ability to choose where to direct your attention.

BOUNDARIES THAT SUPPORT EQUALITY:

- **Get educated on equality**. Learn how inequality and power imbalance may arise in both macro and micro ways (such as in society, in the home, and even within oneself).

- **Engage in practices that harmonize** the different aspects of your relationship. An example would be an equanimity exercise that embraces various emotions—such as sadness, fear, excitement, anger, calmness, etc. Similar to how all colors are inherently equal and valuable to the whole, allowing and equalizing emotions can broaden the spectrum of creative potential, even if a personal preference for certain emotions exists.

- **Cultivate equilibrium** by balancing polarities within yourself. If you lean toward being "soft," "nurturing," and "gentle," actively explore the counter side of that polarity, exploring how you can utilize the qualities of "hard," "firm," and "strong" to align with the truth of your desires more fully. Seek guidance in recognizing biases and creating space for the spectrum of possibilities, enabling you to equalize and utilize the advantages of both sides of polarity.

- **Develop affirmations** that uphold both internal and external equality, such as, "I am no better than my partner, and I am no worse than my partner. I am an equal." Remember that these affirmations are built on top of safety needs or safety boundaries that are already in place.

BOUNDARIES THAT SUPPORT CURIOSITY:

- **Engage in a willingness to question** all of your viewpoints, beliefs, and perspectives. Be willing to engage in self-investigation repeatedly and whenever needed.

- **Dismantle any layers of resistance** you have toward being wrong. Discover the advantages inherent in embracing fallibility and equalize the value of being both right and wrong.

- **Educate yourself** on the science and art of asking creative, powerful, and effective questions through sources like books, question cards, classes, and courses.

- **Enlist reputable coaches or therapists** who can model curiosity and support you in posing more effective questions to yourself and others.

- **Strengthen the more nuanced layers** of safety within the hierarchy of relationship needs, creating an environment where it feels secure to explore challenging questions within yourself and with others.

- **Be conscious of groups**, organizations, or ideologies that assert ultimate truths, claim the sole correct path, or discourage independent research, learning, and scientific exploration beyond the groups' resources.

- **If any subject feels off-limits** or unsuitable for open discussion, seek support to unravel the underlying issues preventing discourse and work toward resolution.

- **Infuse variety into your routine**. Altering your daily habits allows your mind to approach things from fresh angles, fostering new avenues of curiosity and attention. Changing small elements, such as the placement of your shampoo or taking a different route to the store, can influence your capacity to think differently and embrace curiosity.

- **Engage in creative expressions** that can broaden awareness and foster curiosity. For example, engaging with art can help loosen the mind's grip on perceived certainties, encouraging curiosity about things previously taken for granted or considered unchangeable.

BOUNDARIES THAT SUPPORT VULNERABILITY:

- **Become educated on how to** express your experience authentically. Seek out teachers, coaches, books, and resources tailored to instruct and guide you in this skill.

- **Engage in honest communication** with individuals who have willingly consented to hear the unfiltered truth of your experience.

- **Establish or join groups that prioritize** sharing honest thoughts, emotions, sensations, and behaviors. This could include creating agreements in your current relationships and joining coaching groups, therapy groups, authentic relating groups, and retreats.

- **Learn about the difference between** honest sharing and projection. Become educated on the concept of projections, both positive and negative, and learn strategies to manage and explore projections while sharing your inner self or listening to others share their inner world.

- **Get coaching or counseling designed** to help you share in more authentic and productive ways and integrate that sharing into conversations about the "we."

- **Incorporate intentional check-ins** into your routine. Intimacy check-ins help you slow down, connect with the present moment, and communicate from a place of greater awareness.

BOUNDARIES THAT SUPPORT COURAGE:

- **Recognize and acknowledge** your intimacy fears with compassion. Learn to approach these fears without suppressing them, treating them as problems, or allowing them to dictate your decisions.

- **Educate yourself about** the advantages of intimacy. Truly understanding the benefits of intimacy can support you in engaging in intimacy work even when it feels frightening.

- **Understand that feeling fear is** normal and even expected during this phase of relationship growth. Learn to distinguish between fear and genuine evidence of danger or harm.

- **Utilize breathwork**, body practices, and mindfulness techniques to stretch your capacity to remain present amidst the intensified emotional experiences and sensations that may arise during intimate experiences.

- **Take breaks when necessary**. Gauge when you've exceeded your intimacy capacity or need rest. Like practicing a yoga pose, pushing beyond your capacity can lead to injury.

- **Remember that intimacy** development is oriented toward thriving. If safety issues arise (physically or psychologically), take a break from intimacy development and focus on reestablishing safety.

- **Create a consistent routine** for engaging in an intimacy development process. Regular practice will hone your skills, boost your confidence, and offer frequent opportunities to experience intimacy benefits.

- **Seek help, feedback**, coaching, mentorship, and counseling as needed.

- **Establish connections** with practice partners and helpers who can provide the necessary support and encouragement to help you express yourself, even when faced with fear.

INTIMACY FULFILLMENT

At this point, you may be able to discern the distinction between intimacy and friendship, including how the two differ from each other and from the foundational levels of safety in relationships.

While comprehending intimacy as a concept can be very helpful, experiencing intimacy transforms the concept into form, creating a more complete understanding and allowing for its furthered fulfillment.

Intimacy development is one of my particular areas of interest, both personally and professionally.

A portion of this book is dedicated to teaching you the intimacy development model that I created and use in my own life and in my work with clients. I call this the POET process.

Chapter 11
THE POET PROCESS

The POET process is a four-step intimacy development model. The acronym reminds you that you are the poet of your own life. You can, with the POET process, take whatever is happening in and around you, and use it as the ingredients to more fully acknowledge the truth of who you are and create poetic expressions of that reality.

You can also use the POET process in partnership with another to write the poetry of your relationship. When using POET in tandem, together you become the co-authors of something beautiful, meaningful, creative, and co-aligned.

Every close relationship, including your relationship with self, experiences conflict, triggers, and pain points. There are three ways that you navigate these difficulties. You either mask, with any combination of passive or aggressive responses, you show up as the authentic self, or you engage some mix of both.

Relationships limited to Levels One, Two, and Three of the hierarchy will generally respond to conflict, triggers, and pain points with masked responses and coping strategies.

When Level Four desires and needs begin to arise it becomes imperative that one learns how to remove the mask and engage from a more authentic expression of the truth.

When I started piecing together the POET Process, I was contemplating the "how." How do people shift from masked states to embody more and more of their authentic selves at any given moment?

Immersed in studying various coaching and therapeutic models, I became captivated by the common threads I saw running through the different models and what differentiated those threads. I began to discern four fundamental aspects of removing masks and showing up authentically. Every coaching or therapeutic model I have ever learned can be categorized within one or more of these four steps outlined by the four letters of POET.

Along with the importance of these four steps, another foundational realization has been the sequence in which these four steps must be followed.

If I attempted to use a coaching or therapeutic model that focused on Step 3 (the "E" of POET) before a client had adequately attended to Steps 1 and 2 (the "P" and the "O" of POET), our work aimed at "E" was very likely to be ineffective, increase distress, and produce unsatisfactory results.

The benefit of this knowledge has been indispensable in my ability to cultivate intimacy in my own life and consistently do effective work with clients.

In the following chapters, you will learn the four steps of POET.

While reading about each step as a concept is an important first step, the best way to learn the process is to immerse yourself in a consistent practice.

Progressing your ability to use POET is similar to advancing in a sport, subject, or musical instrument. Many situations have nuance, and without support along the way, you are likely to face stuck points and slower progress.

If you want more support and free resources to help you learn and practice the four steps of POET, get your free book bonus at:

www.jennymorrow.com/bookbonus.

Chapter 12
THE "P" IN POET

The POET process is designed to help you cultivate and advance intimacy with yourself and others. Each step of the POET process can be done individually, as you develop intimacy in your self-relationship or with another as you develop intimacy with another person.

P – PRESENCE

The "P" in P.O.E.T. represents *Presence.*

Presence involves directing your attention toward the present moment and fully acknowledging the truth of what is occurring.

Like an enthusiastic puppy that chases anything that catches its eye, our untrained attention becomes hooked by and follows the dramatic narratives arising from our unexamined beliefs.

These often play out as loops of automatic stories that repeat in our heads.

Presence serves as the initial step to becoming conscious of these automatic responses. By slowing down and observing what has your attention, you begin to gain choice in something that was previously outside of your awareness.

There are many teachings designed to support you in developing the skill of presence. Meditation and mindfulness often fit within this step. Even the skill of being able to slow down and notice your breath when a moment of stress or conflict arises can be a practice in presence.

When a therapist asks, "How did you feel about that?" they are asking you to *presence* yourself.

There are many things you can presence—including your own thoughts, emotions, behaviors, and sensations. Additionally, you can presence what is occurring outside of yourself in your surroundings, such as the sunny weather, the tense tone of a child, or the dust on your bookshelves.

Often, the moment you become aware of something that you consider negative, wrong, uncomfortable, problematic, or threatening, it elicits a reactive sensation, a triggered response, or a sense of conflict from within.

This response indicates that you have reached the edges of what I refer to as your *Intimacy Capacity.*

YOUR INTIMACY CAPACITY

Your intimacy capacity represents how much energy you can receive, hold, and give. Energy, in this context, refers to truth or accurate information about reality. This energy can show up in the form of love, health, money, connection, knowledge, skills, and more.

The edges of your intimacy capacity, or your *intimacy limits*, reflect the current constraints on your ability to engage with reality. These limits arise from lack of experience, inaccurate worldviews and beliefs, conditioning that is misaligned with reality, and gaps in knowledge.

The area beyond your intimacy capacity represents the realms of knowledge and understanding that are yet to be explored or comprehended.

Whenever an event, situation, circumstance, or experience occurs, information enters your awareness through your senses (sight, hearing, touch, smell, etc.). This data is then processed through the filter of your beliefs, and you begin to experience sensations, thoughts, emotions, and behaviors. Often, these responses appear so swiftly that you assume they are linked to reality rather than your perception of reality.

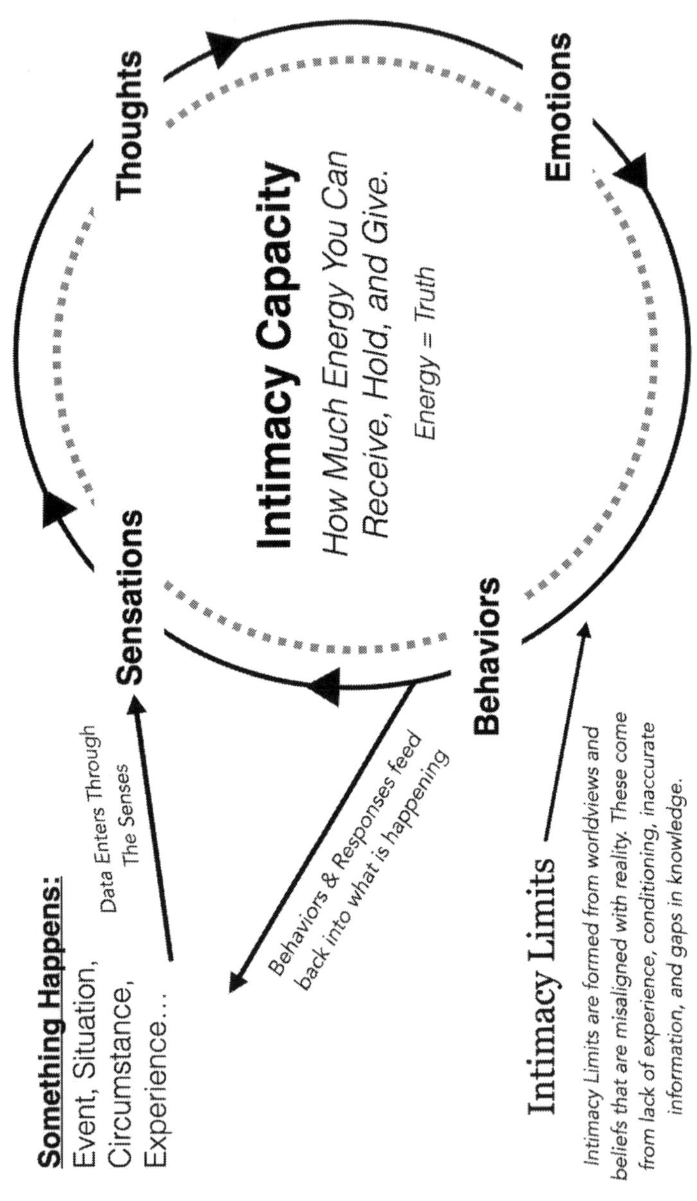

Figure 10 – Intimacy Capacity Illustration

This sequence cycles until you slow down and engage a method such as POET.

The four doorways into your intimacy capacity—sensations, thoughts, emotions, and behaviors—are the four access points through which you can apply the POET process, starting with presence.

While struggles, conflict, and triggers are not always comfortable, one of their great benefits is that they act as an opportunity to expand the edges of your intimacy capacity.

Next time you find yourself triggered, notice the experience of your edge. You may feel it as a zing, rush of energy, surge of heat, tingling in your body, a sudden racing of thoughts, or whooshes of fear, anger, excitement, or confusion.

In such moments, if you are relating from Levels One, Two, or Three in the hierarchy, you will likely enter a state of masking, from which you attempt to address or resolve the trigger or perceived threat through the lens of the masked response.

The POET process, on the other hand, offers an alternative. Rather than simply responding from a mask, you can, with enough safety and proper boundaries in place, engage intimacy, be with what is, and notice your relationship to the experience —through awareness of the four access points.

This doesn't mean that masking never happens. It means that when it does, you slow down, get present, release attachment to maintaining the mask, and instead observe your response, allowing it to give you information about what is needed to get back to center, or into alignment with your truth.

Over time, the practice of Presence allows you the opportunity to more fully know your true self, others, and the world around you, the results of which lead to the ability to reclaim more aspects of the self and further unveil your personal and relational power.

WHAT TO PRESENCE

When you decide to consciously engage POET, as an intimacy practice, during a moment of struggle, stress, or conflict, you can presence three areas specifically:

#1: Presence your *struggle.*
#2: Presence your *desire.*
#3: Presence your *environment.*

Example Scenario: You have just interviewed for the perfect job, and since the interview, you've been feeling anxious about whether or not you'll get the new position. You notice internal conflict as you vacillate between the thoughts, "I hope I get the new job" and "What if I don't get the new job."

The Struggle

The struggle, which can show up as a stress response, tension, or conflict, is the experience of a problem—whether real or perceived. A struggle can be broken down into the vacillation between hope and fear.

PRESENCE THE STRUGGLE:

> *"I hope I get the new job and I feel fear about not getting the new job."*

PRESENCE HOW YOU RELATE TO THE STRUGGLE:

> *"When I feel hope about getting the new job, I feel a relief, a kind of freedom that I would finally be able to do what I really want to do. When I feel afraid that I will not get the job, I obsessively think about it. I get butterflies in my stomach. I wonder whether or not I'm good enough, and I act less patient with my kids."*

The Desire

Desire here is defined as something bigger than the struggle. It is something that transcends the conflict, and can encompass, or hold, both the hope and the fear.

In the example scenario, you might reflect and realize that whether or not you get the new job, you desire to find work you really love.

PRESENCE YOUR DESIRE:

> *"I want to find work I really love."*

PRESENCE HOW YOU RELATE TO YOUR DESIRE:

> *"When I reconnect to my desire, I feel grounded. I feel more*

peace and trust. I imagine that there are many possibilities. I slow down and act more patient with myself and my kids."

The Environment

Your environment encompasses the elements of your surroundings. Noticing aspects of the environment can serve as points of focus or anchors that can ground you in the present moment and provide a sense of stability and connection while you bridge the gap between the experience of your struggle and the reconnection with your desire.

PRESENCE YOUR ENVIRONMENT:

"I am noticing the inhale and exhale of my breath."

Examples of other things you might notice include:

- Your cat's eyes
- The clouds moving outside your child's window
- The sensation of the couch under your body
- The sweetness of the mango you are eating

PRESENCE HOW YOU RELATE TO YOUR ENVIRONMENT:

"When I notice the inhale and exhale of my breath, my shoulders relax, and my mind begins to settle."

AN ADVANCED TIP

Experiencing struggle, or vacillation between hope and fear, does not always manifest as a "negative" sensation or tension. There are instances when it may actually present itself as a seemingly "positive" experience.

For example, rather than feeling afraid that you might not get the job, you may be on a "high," confident that you did so well in the interview that the only possible outcome is getting the job.

Even though the high might feel positive, the challenge lies in the fact that those highs are still associated with misaligned beliefs about yourself and reality.

For example, no matter how good you feel about the interview, a call letting you know you didn't get the job could bring all of your insecurities rushing back in.

As you learn to find balance between the polarities, you will observe that while the "positive" experiences might initially be preferable to the "negative" experiences, they will both feel different than the truth of center—which neither exceeds nor falls short of the truth of your desire nor does it surpass or diminish the reality of who you really are.

For this reason, you can approach the POET process either through the lows or the highs of a struggle, as both will provide valuable insights and opportunities for deepening intimacy.

THE PRIMARY CHALLENGES TO PRESENCE

In my coaching and teaching experience, I have identified two common obstacles that hinder engagement with presence.

One obstacle is the misconception that presence creates reality. Here, one believes that the act of presence can create negative outcomes.

A metaphor here involves my dental hygiene. For years, I would only floss my teeth before brushing. If I had already brushed, I would skip flossing, believing it would introduce debris into my "clean" mouth. It took logical thinking for me to consciously realize that flossing isn't the cause of food particles in my mouth; rather, it reveals their presence. They were already there. I had merely enjoyed the temporary illusion of being unaware of them.

Similarly, it is essential to understand that presence doesn't create reality but rather brings to light the truth of what already exists.

A second common obstacle that hinders engagement with presence is uncertainty about what one will do after achieving it.

Many clients express concern that if they presence difficult thoughts or feelings, they will get stuck in those thoughts or feelings, perhaps indefinitely, without a next step.

Without knowing the subsequent steps of POET, presence can appear frightening. In these situations, you may resist engaging in presence. You may also feel anxious and afraid when you observe others engage in presence.

As you become familiar with all four steps of POET, presence gradually becomes less intimidating to navigate. You see that it is only the first step of a process and that subsequent steps are available to support a more complete resolution.

Once you have sufficiently met the experience of presence, you will be ready to move to the "O" of POET.

Chapter 13
THE "O" IN POET

O – OWNING REALITY WITH COMPASSION

The "O" in POET represents *Owning Reality With Compassion.*

When faced with the discomfort of conflict or struggle, the natural inclination is to seek a swift resolution. This tendency is not necessarily problematic, as the desire to resist pain and pursue pleasure is threaded throughout the human body and has served human evolution in many ways.

However, challenges arise when you encounter triggers, conflicts, or tension and attempt to resolve problems on the surface without truly understanding the underlying issues at play.

In these moments, a hasty attempt at resolution is often filtered through masked responses, unconscious parts of the self, inaccurate worldviews, and misunderstandings about the issue, leading to ineffective solutions and continued suffering.

There are certain signs that can indicate that your resistance to reality or attachment to a prompt resolution is impeding your progress rather than aiding it. These signs include repetitive patterns of struggle, repeatedly encountering similar triggers, an inability to resolve a long-term problem, or being stuck in a masked state.

The "O" in POET is an antidote to this hasty approach by encouraging you to slow down and stay present, as doing so is the only way to engage in the next steps of the process while remaining receptive to new information.

There are two parts to the "O," both of which support you in owning reality with compassion.

Part #1 – Owning Reality:

Here, you embrace accountability for your role in the fabric of existence by firmly holding your sense of self amidst the experience of presence. You adopt a mindset, attitude, and willingness to be fully present in reality, accepting it as it is, even if you're not yet clear about how to change it, process it, or find contentment with it.

If this seems overwhelming, you always have the option to step back into presence and remain there, simply observing your breath, emotions, thoughts, sensations, environment, or the unfolding of the experience.

Part #2 –With Compassion:

The phrase "With Compassion" serves as a reminder to infuse this step with loving-kindness. My definition of compassion is:

Awareness of your own or another's suffering, not with pity or charity, but with a clear seeing eye, loving-kindness, and a willingness to understand and work with what is.

Many individuals fear that offering compassion or validation will cause problems. However, like presence, owning reality with compassion does not generate the struggle or perpetuate adverse circumstances.

If, through presence or owning reality with compassion, it becomes clear how to take effective action, I encourage you to make those changes.

From my perspective, the ability to bring about effective change signifies that you have already embraced reality with compassion, whether consciously or unconsciously.

When you are hungry, you likely address your hunger by preparing food. In this scenario, you naturally own your hunger with compassion, albeit unintentionally. When there is no judgment or resistance toward your hunger, you simply resolve it by having a meal. Here, owning reality with compassion is inherent in the act of eating.

Owning reality with compassion is not a barrier to change; instead, it is a vital aspect of effective action. A deliberate practice of this step is crucial when inherent ownership and compassion are not yet established.

By relinquishing judgments rooted in misaligned expectations of how you, life, or others "should" be, this approach of compassion fosters equanimity—a balanced and steady state of mind that opens the doorway to the next step, the "E" of POET.

While owning reality with compassion is not the ultimate destination, it is an essential step in the process. Without traversing this phase, you may find yourself stuck for extended periods of time, unable to effectively resolve situations or make progress.

THE MISCONCEPTIONS THAT BECOME OBSTACLES

There are a variety of misconceptions that create obstacles to owning reality with compassion. By being aware of these misconceptions you can prevent them from halting your progress.

Misconception: Believing that owning reality with compassion and validating means agreeing with, caving in, conceding, quitting, giving up, or allowing bad behavior.

It's important to understand that owning reality with compassion, validation, and loving-kindness does not entail agreement, giving up, or allowing bad behavior. It does not even signify an understanding of the situation or a readiness to set boundaries or take action. Instead, it is simply a willingness to stay present to what is happening and infuse that presence with compassion.

If you find yourself eating doughnuts despite your intention to adopt a healthier diet, owning reality with compassion does not imply that you are abandoning your desire to be healthy or resigning yourself to a lifetime of doughnut consumption. What it does mean is that right now, at this moment, you are eating doughnuts, and you are willing to be present with yourself in that reality.

Owning reality with compassion is sometimes all that is needed to experience a sudden and seemingly miraculous shift or "waking up." The moment you permit yourself to stay present might be the moment you suddenly feel and know yourself more fully. This connection alone might be enough to create the momentum needed to do more of what you truly desire and less of what you don't. In the doughnut example, there may be a sudden release of the urge to fill yourself with multiple sweet treats.

When owning reality with compassion doesn't inspire immediate change, it does support you in moving forward to the next step of POET, where you will identify what mindsets, missing information, and competing needs might be standing in your way and hindering you from reaching your desires.

Misconception: Believing that because owning reality with compassion doesn't directly get you what you want, it isn't worth your time.

Just as presence is not the ultimate goal of the POET process, owning reality with compassion does not indicate the end of your journey.

Amid a stressful relational moment, your mind may try to convince you to skip this step, arguing that if it's not the magic pill that fixes the problem now, it's not worth your time, but consider the analogy of baking a cake. While cracking an egg and mixing the batter, you wouldn't think, "This isn't working ... I want to eat a cake, not this soup-like batter." Instead, you would recognize that preparing the batter is a necessary step toward your end goal.

Similarly, the "O" of POET is not synonymous with your desired outcome, and at the same time, you can't get to your desired outcome without it. Two more steps follow "O," and you must engage in "O" to reach those steps. Skipping the "O" is like baking a cake without mixing the batter—it won't get you what you want.

Misconception: Believing the opposite of "O" to be true.

Another hindrance to owning reality with compassion is the deeply ingrained belief that to achieve a desired result; you must do the *opposite* of owning reality with compassion.

Examples of this misconception include:

- Believing that to get your child to behave, you must coerce them into agreeing with your values.
- Believing that to attain your desired physical appearance, you need to beat yourself up when you skip a run.
- Believing that to keep a connection with your partner, you must push aside an uncomfortable feeling and maintain a facade of positivity.

If you were modeled a traditional approach to pursuing the life you desire, you were modeled an approach that is limited to the first three levels of the hierarchy and normalizes masking to attain your goals.

The problem is that when you are ready to engage intimacy, the same mask you once wore to "attain your desires" becomes the very barrier that restricts you from moving beyond traditional relationships—relationships that do not develop beyond Level Three—Friendship.

Removing the mask and owning reality with compassion may seem counterintuitive, as it might feel like a departure from what you have been taught and observed in the world around you.

Misconception: Believing that if you own reality with compassion, you'll have to pretend or ignore how you feel

Many individuals mistakenly associate owning reality with compassion with feeling a certain way, specifically feeling calm, peaceful, and relaxed. This misconception can lead to "O" being seen as compatible with pretending, ignoring, or passivity.

While owning reality with compassion can and often does lead to greater peace, that greater sense of peace or acceptance accompanying this step always rides in on the back of truth.

For example, owning reality with compassion doesn't mean ignoring your anger. It means being compassionate with your experience of anger. It doesn't mean hiding your embarrassing thoughts. It means a willingness to work with the truth despite those thoughts.

It is crucial to understand that owning reality with compassion never involves pretense. Instead, it entails being with the truth of the present moment, exactly as it is, with compassion.

Owning reality with compassion ultimately requires an internal shift in your being. You may, at times, have the intention to own reality with compassion while still being riddled with resistance and judgments. In these instances, one thing you can honestly validate is that you cannot yet own something with compassion, *"I cannot yet own my child's fear with compassion."* That is owning reality with compassion!

SUPPORTIVE PHRASES

While owning reality with compassion is ultimately a state of being, I have discovered the importance of utilizing tools to help you align with this step.

One of the most helpful tools for this step is *supportive phrases.* Supportive phrases serve as guides, helping you flex and stretch your owning reality with compassion muscles.

There are a variety of supportive phrases you can use. I have included a few examples of the phrases that I frequently use. You may also create your own.

No Wonder___(fill in the blank)___.

- "No wonder I am feeling afraid."
- "No wonder my husband didn't pay our bill on time."
- "No wonder I have a headache."
- "No wonder my child is biting other children."

- "No wonder I want to scroll on social media."

While I don't always have insight into the underlying reasons and causes behind a situation, the phrase "No wonder" reminds me that just like the test tube in a lab will showcase a perfect reaction to its contents, life perfectly reflects what each moment contains.

Remembering this reminds me that there is a reason that things are as they are, that what I'm experiencing may not be as personal as it feels, and that there are many components to each moment, many of which are beyond my comprehension.

"Even though__(fill in the blank)__, I deeply and completely honor and love myself."

- "Even though my spouse feels irritated, I completely care about them."
- "Even though I forgot to get eggs at the grocery store, I deeply respect myself."
- "Even though my coworker is pessimistic, I fully honor them."
- "Even though I spoke harshly with my child, I deeply love myself, and am willing to figure out what's going on with me."

The phrase "Even though" is a powerful reminder that despite the complexities of any given moment, you can reorient and ground your core intention in care and respect for yourself and others.

"This is what it's like to___(fill in the blank)___"

- "This is what it's like to feel annoyed."
- "This is what it's like to believe my child doesn't appreciate me."

This phrase can also be a question:

- "What was it like for you when I told you I had made a big purchase without consulting you?"

This phrase acknowledges your willingness to know and be with what is happening in the moment rather than resisting it.

"I give myself permission to experience ______(fill in the blank)___ for as long as I need to."

- "I give myself permission to feel flat and depressed as long as I need to."
- "I give my partner permission to be worried about money for as long as they need to."
- "I give my boss permission to micromanage things for as long as she needs to."

This supportive phrase aims to help you embrace reality as it truly is by relieving yourself and others of unproductive pressure to conform to idealized expectations of how things "should be." Here, you encourage trust in what is.

"Just because ____(fill in the blank)____doesn't mean it will always be that way."

- "Just because I feel afraid to take the next step in my business doesn't mean I'll always feel afraid."
- "Just because my spouse is distracted by their phone doesn't mean they'll always be distracted by their phone."
- "Just because my daughter feels left out at school doesn't mean she'll always feel left out."

This supportive phrase emphasizes that the current state of affairs may not be as permanent as it appears and could change at any time. By allowing yourself to make space for the possibility of change, you also gain more ability to be with what is in the moment.

OWNING STRUGGLES AND DESIRES WITH COMPASSION

Similar to presence, when you are consciously engaging the POET process to navigate conflict and struggle, I suggest owning three things with compassion, specifically:

#1: Own the struggles and conflict with compassion.
#2: Own your desires with compassion.
#3: Own the environment with compassion.

You can apply supportive phrases to any of these three areas to help you stay present and connected with reality amidst struggle.

Own struggles and conflicts with compassion

Here, you own the struggles and conflict, and their accompanying sensations, thoughts, emotions, and behaviors, with compassion.

- Even though I long for my boss's approval, I deeply and completely love and accept myself.
- I give myself permission to be in conflict with my spouse and to feel frustrated.
- No wonder I am overspending and feel nervous about my financial situation.

Own your desires with compassion

Remember that true desires are bigger than the present struggle or conflict. When accessed, these desires can hold both the hope and fear underlying the struggle.

- This is what it's like to desire to know I am enough, no matter what others, including my boss, think of me.
- Even though my spouse and I are in conflict, I trust this process will help us to understand ourselves and each other more fully.
- I give myself permission to learn what it will really take to create financial freedom.

Own the environment with compassion

By owning the environment with compassion, you allow these focal points to support you in staying present to aspects of what is happening.

- Even though all I can do is breathe right now, I deeply respect myself.
- No wonder I like to watch the clouds drift by my window.
- This is what it's like to notice the sensation of the floor under my feet.
- I give myself permission to enjoy the sweetness of this mango.

A DOORWAY

Owning reality with compassion is a doorway. It keeps the door to presence open. Once you have sufficiently embraced the experience of owning reality with compassion, you will be prepared to proceed to the "E" in POET.

Chapter 14
THE "E" IN POET

E – EXPLORATION

The "E" in POET represents *Exploration*. Exploration refers to the examination and investigation of both your inner and outer worlds. It often includes a journey into and through less known aspects of yourself, life, and others.

Because intimacy widens the focus from survival to thriving, it begins to question the gaps between the experience of suffering and genuine desire. At this stage, you explore various facets of perceived problems by posing questions that offer a more complete inquiry into the space between struggle and creating the outcomes you desire.

These inquiries are driven by curiosity and a willingness to transcend limited perspectives. They encourage you to expand the boundaries of your intimacy capacity, enabling a more accurate perception of reality. Through these investigations, you better understand the situation, allowing for more effective solutions.

In my early years as a therapist, I worked in the addiction field. Many of my clients and their families held onto a belief that went something like this: *"A good person wouldn't give up their family for their addiction."*

However, I learned something that profoundly impacted my life during that time. I observed that addiction is not a moral issue; it's not about good or bad. Instead, addiction is a processing issue. It's the inability to process reality accurately—specifically, the failure to comprehend (at least consciously) what actions will lead to what outcomes.

I now firmly believe that this applies to all patterns of suffering. The factors that lead to suffering are not moral issues; they are processing issues. They stem from the inability to process how to create the life and the relationships you desire. Without a clear picture of reality—masked responses, addictions, and other forms of suffering, all of which rely on fantasies to be maintained—arise as strategies that ultimately prove ineffective.

Exploration includes a gradual unveiling of the true origins of suffering, the ability to distinguish fact from fiction, and the opportunity to surpass limitations, unleash the power of boundaries, and take effective action.

Consequently, problems no longer appear as insurmountable obstacles and instead lose their grip or dissolve effortlessly.

LOGIC AND EMOTION

When you are in exploration, understanding and integrating two significant concepts—logic and emotion—is crucial.

Logic: Logic is the process of engaging accurate reasoning. It encompasses the precise handling of information about objective facts and external phenomena. Logic includes adherence to principles of reliability and validity. Logic requires that you extend your attention and focus outward, acting as an energy-out practice.

Emotion: Emotion, including its expression as thoughts and sensations, represents a subjective experience that offers you information regarding the truth of your inner world. Emotion requires you to receive what is arising as an energy-in experience.

Your encounter with reality is where your inner and outer worlds meet. For this reason, both logic and emotion are equally vital to creating an aligned life. By creating a more accurate process of logic, energy-out, you can induce a change in your emotional experience, energy-in.

EDUCATION ON CRITICAL THINKING

Learning sound logic is a skill. Because exploration utilizes logic, it can help to have some education on critical thinking skills. There are a variety of *ineffective* approaches to logic that break down effective critical thinking.

Three categories of obstacles that stand in the way of effective logic are:

- Cognitive Bias
- Thinking Errors or Cognitive Distortions
- Logical Fallacies

Cognitive Bias:

Cognitive bias is the tendency to favor or avoid a particular logical outcome due to emotional influence, personal preference, past choices, and other factors. This bias hinders impartiality and prevents adequate consideration of evidence from all perspectives. Typically, this bias operates unconsciously.

One example of cognitive bias is the *Spotlight Effect.* The spotlight effect is a bias that leads one to assume that others notice them more than they do.

Another common cognitive bias is the *Confirmation Bias*. This bias refers to the inclination to seek out, understand, prioritize, and remember information in a manner that aligns with your preexisting beliefs or values.

Numerous cognitive biases have been identified and documented. A simple internet search on *cognitive bias* will bring up an abundance of examples.

At the time of writing, I came across an extensive list of cognitive biases.

See the URL for this list in the references at the back of book ("List of Cognitive Biases," 2023).

Thinking Errors (also known as cognitive distortions):

Thinking errors are errors in logic that result in distorted perceptions of reality and illogical conclusions. While cognitive biases relate to how emotional influence can impact one's logical process, thinking errors refer to an inaccurate approach to processing.

Although cognitive biases are one of the main contributors to thinking errors, these errors can also stem from conditioned approaches to logical analysis, lack of education, limited skills in critical thinking, lazy reasoning, previous modeling, or fatigue and stress. Often, thinking errors are experienced automatically and assumed to be true.

One example of a thinking error is a *should—"they should, he should, I should..." Shoulds* are thinking errors that revolve around a subjective decision someone has made about how life, themselves, or others ought to be and respond. *Shoulds* are generally defined before engaging in a thorough exploration of reality.

You can also do an internet search on *thinking errors* or *cognitive distortions,* and you will find many examples. At the time of this writing, I found a webpage that lists 15 common cognitive distortions with specific examples.

See the URL for this webpage in the references at the back of book ("Understanding and Overcoming Cognitive Distortions," 2023).

Logical Fallacies:

A logical fallacy occurs when invalid or flawed reasoning is employed in the development of an argument, making it appear well-reasoned unless one recognizes the error. I have found that these logical fallacies are not only used in developing arguments with others but also in developing arguments that you have with yourself.

A common logical fallacy is a false dilemma. A false dilemma presents two perspectives, extending them as the only two possibilities that exist in a situation when, in fact, there are more options.

Many logical fallacies have been identified. An internet search on logical fallacies will bring up many examples. At the time of this writing, I found a large list of logical fallacies.

See the URL for this list in the references at the back of book ("List of Fallacies," 2023).

EDUCATE YOURSELF

Take time to visit the websites referenced above (they can be found in the reference section towards the end of the book) or do your own research and reading on critical thinking skills. Becoming more educated in logical reasoning creates a stronger foundation for the step of exploration. The goal is not that these biases, distortions, and fallacies never happen because they likely will. The goal is that you learn to catch them when they do happen or soon after. Seeing these obstacles for what they are allows you to explore more effectively, with a better chance of aligning your awareness with reality.

THE LOGIC OF EMOTIONS

Logic and emotions are two sides of a polarity, and while each side serves a different function, they are not separable. Your emotions will inform what logic you prioritize, and the logic of your emotions will guide you in your journey toward inner truth.

During reactivity, suffering, or triggers, these two aspects, emotion and logic, often become enmeshed, blurring their distinctions, or they polarize, giving rise to the illusion of conflicting forces.

For several years, I lived in the foothills of the Rocky Mountains, often venturing onto hiking trails that rattlesnakes call home. While I saw a few snakes over the years, it was much more common to have run-ins with something resembling rattlesnakes but much less dangerous...squiggly sticks.

During my run-ins with squiggly sticks, my heart would leap as if I saw a real rattlesnake, and a surge of fear would wash over me. Whether it was a rattlesnake or a stick looking back at me, my emotional response was the same.

Frequently, we blur the boundaries and mistakenly assume that our emotions accurately reflect external truth. When we hold this expectation, emotions can appear untrustworthy and unreliable.

In the book *Thinking, Fast and Slow,* author Daniel Kahneman underscores the scientific evidence demonstrating the unreliability of emotion and intuition when evaluating logical reality. This unreliability holds especially true in areas and subjects to which you have not devoted ample time applying a precise, logical process (Kahneman, 2011).

While emotions are not reliable indicators of facts, they are extremely reliable indicators of something logical facts are not —the truth of your internal world.

An area of personal and professional interest has been identifying the language of emotions and how emotions provide valid and reliable insights. One way your emotions offer invaluable information is that you can always trust your emotions to reveal your beliefs.

For instance, fear does not reliably indicate danger, but it does reliably signify a *belief* that you perceive that something you value can be threatened.

Drawing upon this understanding, I have developed some emotional "hacks."

Envision yourself as a hired hacker assigned to access a data system represented by the belief patterns that define the edges of your intimacy capacity. Your task is to uncover the system's limitations or inaccurate beliefs and reveal them to your own awareness.

In such situations, emotional hacks involve utilizing charged emotions, thoughts, and sensations to expedite and enhance your access to the data system. In this situation, emotions serve as a reliable tool to gain insights into your worldviews and beliefs more swiftly and effectively.

EMOTIONAL HACKS

The following list outlines a range of emotions, accompanied by a reliable and valid interpretation for each.

SHAME – *Shame informs you that you* ***believe*** *you are fundamentally flawed and cannot have something you want.*

Shame does not indicate a misalignment between your actions, authentic self, or genuine desires. Evaluating whether or not there is a misalignment requires logic.

For example, you might feel shame even when your actions align with your honest values and genuine desires, or, on the flip side, you might feel shameless despite showing up in a way that is completely misaligned with who you want to be.

GUILT – *Guilt lets you know that you* ***believe*** *you did something wrong or made a bad choice.*

Guilt does not imply that you have done something wrong or made a choice that is misaligned with your authentic self or real desires. Evaluating whether or not that is true in reality requires a logical analysis.

CONTEMPT – *Contempt informs you that you **believe** someone else is fundamentally flawed and somehow capable of keeping you from what you want.*

Contempt is similar to shame but directed outward. Contempt does not imply that someone is inferior to you or that their actions are misaligned with their values, your values, or either of your genuine desires. Evaluating such alignment requires logical evaluation.

GUILT-TRIPPING – *Guilt-tripping (as an emotional experience) lets you know that you **believe** someone else is making a bad or wrong choice.*

Guilt-tripping is similar to guilt but directed outward. This outward sense that someone should make another choice does not necessarily indicate that another's choice is misaligned with their values, your values, or either of your genuine desires. Evaluating this requires logical analysis.

SADNESS – *Sadness lets you know that you are releasing and letting go of an old story.*

Sadness does not signify that what you perceive to be lost is indeed lost. Evaluating the truth about loss requires a logical assessment.

If, beyond the narrative that is being released with sadness lies a more accurate awareness of reality, sadness carries a sense of purification, release, relief, and connection. However, if on the other side of sadness lies another untrue story about oneself, the other side of sadness might feel dark, bleak, helpless, hopeless, or frightening.

ANGER – *Anger lets you know that you are* ***believing*** *a self-betraying belief. Specifically, a belief that goes against the truth of who you are and what you are capable or deserving of.*

Anger does not imply that someone has done something to hurt, betray, take advantage of, or mistreat you. Evaluating such situations requires logical analysis.

FEAR – *Fear reveals you* ***believe*** *that something you value can be threatened.*

Fear does not indicate the presence of an actual threat. Evaluating the existence of a threat requires logical evaluation.

CONFUSION – *Confusion informs you that you lack sufficient information or awareness to comprehend or attain clarity about a particular matter.*

Confusion does not indicate a problem. It does not indicate whether or not someone is purposefully attempting to confuse you, and it is not an indicator of whether or not there is a solution to a particular problem. Assessing these things requires data and logical reasoning.

JEALOUSY – *Jealousy indicates that you* ***believe*** *you are less valuable, less deserving, or less worthy of something or someone than another.*

Jealousy does not imply the truth of what you desire or whether or not your desire is available or unavailable. If someone or something is unavailable, jealousy does not indicate the reason for the unavailability. Evaluating those things requires a logical process.

ENVY – *Envy identifies that you **believe** you cannot attain a particular thing.*

Envy is not a reliable indicator of your desires or whether or not you can attain a particular thing. It would take logic to assess that.

EXCITEMENT – *Excitement reflects that you are progressing toward a more true **belief**.*

Excitement does not imply that what is happening is aligned with your values or the outcome you truly desire. Assessing such alignment requires logical evaluation.

FREEDOM – *Freedom, as an emotional experience, signifies that you **believe** something that aligns with your inner sovereignty.*

The feeling of freedom does not indicate whether or not something is contributing to your external experience of sovereignty. Assessing that reality requires logical reasoning.

PEACE – *Peace signifies that you **believe** in something aligned with the reality of your inner safety.*

Peace does not reflect whether or not your outer experience is aligned with the safety you desire. Assessing that would take logical analysis.

JOY – *Joy indicates that you **believe** a truth about yourself.*

Joy does not mean that what you are experiencing "out there" is aligned with your external desires. Clarifying that would require logical evaluation.

THE POWER OF EMOTIONS AND LOGIC

Emotions reliably serve as indicators of beliefs—no more and no less. While emotions do not reliably gauge external reality, they reflect an accurate portrayal of inner reality.

Beliefs become flexible when brought into conscious awareness. The advantage of this is that it presents an opportunity to more fully align your beliefs with reality, enabling you to work with what is and create more of what you genuinely desire.

When paired together in exploration, emotions, which give information about the internal world, and logic, which offers information about the external world, provide a broader, more precise picture of the truth.

PREPARING FOR EXPLORATION

It is vital that POET, or any other intimacy development process, is supported by a foundation of safety and friendship.

When that foundation is sufficient, exploration will help you more fully align with reality and hone your ability to stand up for what you desire and value.

If the foundation is insufficient, exploration can cause injury, leading you to discredit reality or facilitate unhealthy behavior. Just like you would not do yoga on an injured leg, do not engage exploration without a good foundation or if it is causing harm.

I have watched people use exploration to punish themselves, put up with bad behavior, or stay stuck. I have also observed unhealthy relationships and high-demand groups use exploration techniques to control others and avoid taking responsibility.

Examples of situations in which exploration can be harmful include:

- Believing you must push yourself into exploration even if you feel tired or need a break.
- Believing that something is wrong with you if you do not trust a particular person to guide you in exploration.
- Using exploration to blame a victim or to pardon a perpetrator of accountability.
- Using exploration to coerce or control another, including yourself.
- Being told that someone else's exploration experience is correct for you because they have access to God or divine messages, and you don't.
- Believing that you are supposed to lean into exploration even if it's feeling off, misaligned, painful, or uncomfortable in an unhealthy way.

Even though a saw is an excellent tool for building a house, it can hurt someone if used carelessly or maliciously. Similarly, the tools used for exploration can cause harm or break down safety when used unskillfully, maliciously, or without the appropriate safety precautions.

If you have concerns about exploration or any step of the POET process, please get support, second opinions, or assessments when needed.

At times, safety and friendship needs are sufficiently established, but exploration still feels unhelpful. When this happens, it likely indicates that you are attempting to move through the POET process too quickly.

One of the most common struggles I see when people use the POET process is ignoring the basics, skipping steps, or moving too fast. Making these mistakes is easy to do when you want to feel better quickly, but you must follow the steps and work from the truth of where you are.

Just like you cannot skip steps when baking a cake or stabilizing a yoga pose, you cannot bypass the "P" and "O" of POET and hope for good results during steps "E" and "T." If you're feeling stuck, back it up a step or two, and see if that helps.

When safety and friendship are sufficiently established, and you have adequately engaged in presence and owning reality with compassion, you are prepared for exploration.

THE 4 STAGES OF EXPLORATION

During exploration, the "E" of POET, you specifically explore the alignment between your beliefs and reality. Here, you use emotions and logic to access a more accurate picture of your point of consciousness, the place where your inner and outer worlds meet.

There are four phases of exploration:

1. ACCESS AND IDENTIFY A BELIEF
2. ENGAGE IN QUESTIONING THE BELIEF
3. EXPLORE THE OPPOSITES
4. ATTEND TO LINKS

1. ACCESS AND IDENTIFY A BELIEF OR STRESSFUL THOUGHT

During the initial phase of exploration, the goal is to access and identify your beliefs. Identifying stressful thoughts or uncomfortable emotions is often the easiest way to do this.

EXAMPLE SCENARIO: Lily is attempting to assist her husband in hanging a painting. She senses that he is annoyed. "Hold the right corner up more," he snaps. In response, she feels waves of heat and notices the emotion of frustration. She thinks, "I'm trying to help, and he doesn't appreciate me."

The stressful thought in this example is:

"I'm trying to help someone who doesn't appreciate me."

2. ENGAGE IN QUESTIONING THE BELIEF OR STRESSFUL THOUGHT

Once you have identified a stressful thought or underlying belief, there are a variety of questions that you can use to explore it:

- How much of me believes the thought, 0–100%?
- What is it like when I'm believing this thought?
- How do I relate to myself and others when I am believing this thought?
- Where have I heard this thought, belief, or idea before?
- When have I believed the opposite of this thought?
- What are the "benefits" of believing this thought?
- What are the impacts of believing this thought?
- What images arise when I believe this thought?
- What memories occur when I believe this thought?
- Do I experience any cravings or destructive desires when I believe this thought?
- How much of me wants to maintain this thought, 0–100%?
- What am I afraid will happen if I do not believe this thought?
- In what ways does this thought protect me?
- What would be different if this thought didn't exist?

The goal of exploration is not to fix reality or to pretend, ignore, or deny it. Instead, exploration is designed to help you see a fuller picture of reality, including how your thoughts and beliefs impact yourself and the situation and how they may or may not align with reality. Even if the stressful thought is true, exploration allows you to look at what else is also true.

Lily poses some of the questions listed above to her stressful thought, *"I'm trying to help someone who doesn't appreciate me."*

She sees that while not being appreciated is a painful experience for her, that pain is exacerbated by how the thought of being unappreciated impacts her.

For example, when she believes that her husband doesn't appreciate her, she becomes less kind to herself and begins to question her own value.

3. EXPLORE THE OPPOSITES

Opposites are the original statements, stressful thoughts, or underlying beliefs flipped inside out.

During this phase of exploration, you use opposites to identify blind spots and angles of reality that were previously out of awareness. This allows you to gain more information, balance your thinking, increase awareness, and be open to new perspectives.

To accomplish this, you use statements that identify the opposites of the thought, belief, idea, or perspective.

Original Example Thought:

"I'm trying to help someone who doesn't appreciate me."

Opposites of the Original Thought:

- I'm trying to help someone who does appreciate me.
- I'm trying to help someone who I don't appreciate.
- I'm trying to help someone and don't appreciate myself.

Here, you notice evidence for the opposites, explicitly paying attention to any opposites that strike a chord. You list examples of ways that the opposites might be as accurate or even more accurate than the initial thought. If an opposite specifically resonates, take time with it and list 2 to 4 pieces of evidence for why that opposite is true.

In Lily's example, she can quickly see the reality that most of the time her husband does appreciate her, and that in this moment, she doesn't appreciate him, or the way he spoke with her. However, it's the opposite, *"I don't appreciate myself,"* that strikes a chord. Here, she lists three examples highlighting the way that this opposite holds some truth:

- "When my husband doesn't appreciate my efforts, I stop seeing the intention of my care, I stop appreciating myself, and I start wondering if something is wrong with me."
- "I am continually focused on what others need, to the point that I often forget myself and ignore what I need."
- "I believe that if I am not helping someone, I don't deserve to be happy. I don't know how to appreciate myself just as I am."

As Lily lists out the evidence of the opposite, she sees that while it's healthy to expect kindness and appreciation from her husband, it's also important to foster kindness and appreciation within herself.

4. ATTEND TO LINKS

In exploration, you explore the stressful thoughts and subconscious beliefs that arise during struggle and conflict. Exploration aims to support you in seeing enough truth to balance back to center. Remember that center represents alignment with your true self and unmasked desires.

In Lily's example, the initial stressful thought was, *"I'm trying to help someone who doesn't appreciate me."* In a situation where this initial stressful thought is the only link, Lily balances her thinking with the discovery that she also struggles to appreciate herself.

Here, Lily decides that while appreciation from her husband holds significance, she wants it to be the icing on the cake of her self-appreciation. This awareness reminds her that she has the power to create more of what she wants, even in the moments when her husband does not appreciate her. When she sees this she feels more connected, safe, and at peace.

From this centered, self-intimate place, Lily approaches her husband without projecting all of her need to be appreciated onto him. He has softened and acknowledges the harsh tone he used with her. He opens up about his insecurity that he was spending time hanging a painting instead of finishing a project for work. Lily shares what she has learned about her need for appreciation from both him and herself.

Despite this struggle, Lily and her husband feel more connected, alive, and secure. They both see themselves and each other more clearly.

At this point, there may or may not be further links to explore. Sometimes, gaining insight into one link is enough to re-center. Other times, the initial stressful thought may only scratch the surface of imbalanced thinking or misaligned beliefs. Further feelings of struggle or pain will arise when that's the case, revealing deeper layers of misaligned beliefs. I call these links.

Let's return to Lily's example and look at what happens when resolving the initial link doesn't complete the reconnection.

Here, Lily follows an exploration of the first link. However, instead of feeling fully resolved, she notices stirrings of another pain.

Beginning the POET process again to attend to the second link, Lily goes deeper and asks herself, *"If I'm not appreciated by myself or others, then what?"* As she sits with the question, an answer emerges: *"If I'm not appreciated, it means I'm not good."*

She realizes that when her husband snapped at her, she felt sad and believed she was not good. At this point, Lily experiences a wave of grief as she visualizes instances where she has taken on excessive responsibilities to maintain the identity of being a "good woman."

This second link provides insight into a deeper struggle that begins to lighten as she owns it with compassion. This link takes more time to navigate as she allows herself to be with the grief and explore what it's been like to carry this belief for so much of her life.

When ready, Lily shares her experience with her husband, inviting him to join her as she explores the opposites. She cries as she turns the thought around, "I am a good person," she says. Together, they list out evidence of her genuine goodness. She begins to feel more relaxed and energized.

When you have sufficiently explored links, you will notice a shift as you see the truth more clearly and come back into alignment.

Clients and students have used the following phrases to describe their experience following the resolution of a link or a series of links:

- *It feels like I just got plugged back in.*
- *It's like I'm waking up.*
- *I reconnected with my inner knowing.*
- *A light is turning on.*
- *I'm doing the work that really matters.*
- *I feel more loving of myself and others.*
- *I can suddenly relax with ease.*
- *I feel more clean inside.*
- *I have more space and freedom.*
- *I feel like I just clicked back into place.*
- *I'm back in flow.*
- *I feel more grounded.*

These completions signify that you have reclaimed an aspect of truth and may be ready to move to the "T" of POET.

Chapter 15
THE "T" IN POET

T – TAKE ACTION

The "T" in POET represents *Take Action*. In the realm of intimacy, the purpose of action is to align with center.

When you struggle with alignment, swaying in and out of masked states, action is used to counterbalance that sway and bring you back to center. From here, you can further express the manifestation of your desire.

While exploration helps you see the truth, action allows you to apply the truth. Taking action is the final step of POET.

When faced with struggle or conflict, most people's first response is, "What do I do? How do I fix this?" Here, conflict, friction, triggers, and differences are flagged as threats that need immediate action. The problem is that, in these moments, your ideas for resolution are likely nothing more than masked responses dressed up like good ideas.

The reality is that most people are never taught to *be with* relational discomfort long enough to engage in intimacy-building, through which you can approach discomfort, discord, and difference as an opportunity to take off your mask and respond to yourself and others from a more honest place.

When you engage action from the "T" of POET, you are not repeating what doesn't work. You are not perpetuating the same patterns that created fertile ground for the struggle to emerge in the first place. Instead, you are making moves that reveal the truth and remove the mask, not reinforce it.

Just like there are two primary sides of masking, passive and aggressive, there are two primary sides of action you can use to balance back to center—initiating and releasing actions.

Initiating actions are the things you DO to create more of what you want. They are a counterbalance to the passive side of masking. Examples include cleaning your closet, calling a friend, eating vegetables, or sharing a feeling.

Releasing actions are the things you DON'T DO to create more of what you want. They involve a conscious choice to opt out of a specific behavior and are a counterbalance to the aggressive side of masking. Examples include refraining from criticizing, not calling someone, not eating something, and not giving advice.

Just like there are four configurations of masking—fight, flight, freeze, and fawn—there are four combinations from which you can take action.

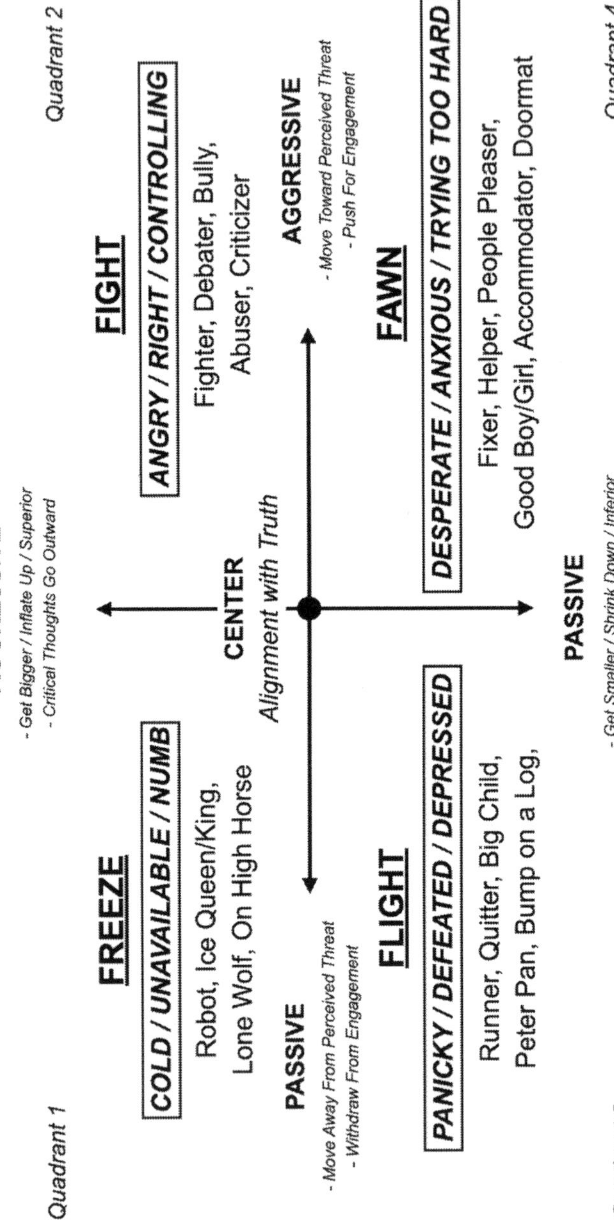

Figure 11 – The Four Configurations of Masking

Counterbalance to the FREEZE response

A releasing/initiating action. For example, you *get off your high horse* (releasing action) and *speak up honestly* (initiating action).

Counterbalance to the FIGHT response

A releasing/releasing action. Here, you *drop your metaphorical weapon* (releasing action) and *stop trying to change someone's mind* (releasing action).

Counterbalance to the FLIGHT response

An initiating/initiating action. Here, you *step into your power* (initiating response) and *speak up honestly* (initiating response).

Counterbalance to the FAWN response

A releasing/initiating action. Here, you *stop trying to fix* (releasing) and *show up as an equal* (initiating).

The details of what each counterbalance will look like depend on the situation's unique specifics.

Rather than using more concepts to illustrate action, I have incorporated examples demonstrating the complete POET process, including the step of taking action.

EXAMPLES OF THE POET PROCESS IN ACTION

Developing intimacy and using the POET process is both a science and an art. Through the POET process, many outcomes can be revealed.

One person's process might lead them to choosing to go to graduate school, while another person's process might lead to the choice to quit graduate school.

The following examples are not meant to illustrate the "right" way but *one* way. The goal is to demonstrate the *process*, not tell you what outcome to choose in each scenario.

Another critical point to remember before reading the following examples is that there is a difference between engaging POET through individual work and engaging it in tandem with another in partner work.

In the realm of individual work, you can use the POET process to expand your intimacy capacity and self-awareness in relationship to yourself and how you perceive others.

In the realm of partner work (such as with a spouse, family member, or business partner), you can use the POET process together, in tandem, to expand the intimacy capacity of your relationship and your ability to collaborate and work together.

In the examples below, I will illustrate the use of POET as a boundary in both individual and partner intimacy work.

EXAMPLE #1 – Kaitlyn Facing the Truth

The following is an example of a woman named Kaitlyn using the POET process to get more aligned in her self-relationship and to clarify the boundaries she will use to support a higher level of safety in her relationship with her husband, Phil.

THE SCENARIO:

Kaitlyn and Phil have been married for six years and have begun to discuss the possibility of having children. In the last year, Kaitlyn has noticed an escalation of intensity in her fights with Phil. There has been yelling and harsh words. Today, he grabbed her by the shoulders and held her while yelling something unkind. She froze and went quiet.

After that Kaitlyn didn't respond. She left the room and began to move through the POET process.

NOTE: Kaitlyn has been doing individual, personal work with a life coach. She has developed a secure enough relationship with herself to engage in an intimacy development process, such as POET, in her self-relationship.

PRESENCE – P

Kaitlyn begins by presencing what just happened.

> *"He grabbed my shoulders and held me while yelling at me."*

She presences how she responded:

> *"I froze. I felt terrified. I still feel terrified and also a bit numb."*

She then presences her inner struggle (the vacillation between her hope and fear):

> *"I hope he can see how much potential we have to be a happy couple and that he will stop blowing up at me. I fear he won't get it; it will happen again, and I will keep letting it happen."*

Next, she presences her desire (bigger than both the hope and the fear, meaning it can encompass both, and generally within one's realm of personal power):

> *"Whether or not Phil can see the problem and change, I want to have a safe partnership where I feel secure."*

OWNING REALITY WITH COMPASSION – O

Despite feeling sad, hurt, and heartbroken, Kaitlyn has enough inner security to own reality with compassion:

> *"Even though this has happened, I deeply and completely honor and love myself."*

As she does this, she notices a thought rise in the background of her mind: *"Maybe he was just having a really rough day. Maybe it won't ever happen again."*

EXPLORATION – E

Kaitlyn has been practicing presence and catches the thought, *"Maybe it won't ever happen again."* She takes this thought into exploration.

"What is it like when I'm believing the thought, 'Maybe it won't ever happen again?'"

> *"I notice a spark of hope. I feel excited and imagine that maybe I can just ignore what happened."*

Kaitlyn begins to have memories of all the times she responded to Phil's verbal aggression by freezing, brushing it under the rug, hoping it would change, and ignoring the hurtful words and the impact they had.

She can now see that her approach has never resolved anything. And today, for the first time, it escalated into physical aggression.

She takes the thought, *"Maybe it won't ever happen again,"* and turns it around to look at its opposite:

> *"Maybe it will happen again."*

She immediately knows that, based on their pattern as a couple and how things have escalated, there is plenty of evidence that this could happen again. She then notices another thought arise:

> *"What if he leaves me?"*

This thought is an example of a link, another layer of thinking that has been associated with her part of the pattern, the fear of abandonment.

She takes this link, this next thought, through the process of exploration using the following questions:

Question 1:

"What images arise when I believe the thought, 'What if he leaves me?'"

> *"I see myself all alone. I wonder whether I'll ever have a child. I imagine that I'll never find another partner. I feel sad because there are so many good things about our relationship."*

Question 2:

"In what ways does the thought, 'What if he leaves me?' protect me?"

> *Thinking this thought has allowed me to downplay what was happening. I assumed that if could focus exclusively on the good, Phil would see how much I care and he would work to be a better husband. I now see that believing this thought didn't protect me. Instead, it has hurt me.*

Question 3:

"What would be different if the thought, 'What if he leaves me?' couldn't come into my mind?"

> *I would focus on what I need to feel safe and secure in this relationship. I would speak up for my needs and hold boundaries.*

Kaitlyn then turns this link around and lays out the opposites to the thought, *"What if he leaves me?"*:

- *"What if he doesn't leave me?"*
- *"What if I leave him?"*
- *"What if I leave me?"*

The last two opposites resonate, and Kaitlyn feels herself click into center. She realizes that her silence following their escalated fights has been a leaving of both herself and the truth of their relationship.

She feels a rising of emotion—both sadness and happiness—the sadness feels cleansing, a letting go of the story that she must stay silent to stay connected. This release is backed by the knowing that she still exists and can return to herself.

TAKE ACTION – T

Kaitlyn decides she is ready to take action and stand up for her physical and psychological safety. If Phil chooses to leave her, that is his choice. She no longer wants to abandon herself or the reality of their relationship—by going silent and not speaking up for her needs.

Kaitlyn makes a same-day appointment with a therapist. In this meeting, she clarifies what she needs for sufficient and ample evidence of safety in this relationship. She lays out a list of written requests.

These requests include the following:

- Either she or Phil will be in a different home until they have received professional support to determine if or when it is safe to be in the same house again.
- Phil will participate in a domestic violence course.
- Both she and Phil will work with individual therapists who are educated on emotional abuse, physical abuse, and power dynamics in relationships.
- When it is determined to be safe enough, they will begin couple work in sessions that include both of their therapists. These sessions will assess physical and psychological safety, track progress, and teach healthy communication skills and conflict management.
- Together with their therapists, they will create a support team that includes a few family members and friends with whom safety issues can be shared immediately. The therapists will give this support team some basic-level training on supporting both her and Phil at this time.

Here is a breakdown for you, the reader, of Kaitlyn's boundary structure:

Kaitlyn's first boundary was an intimacy boundary that she applied in her self-relationship. It was a choice to engage the POET process and get more honest with herself.

Through her engagement with the POET process Kaitlyn was able to clarify her personal requests, as listed above.

The next boundary is a safety boundary that she unilaterally sets with herself. This boundary is that she will only talk with Phil once a professional witness is present.

Not knowing whether Phil will comply with her requests, she establishes a third safety boundary. If Phil cannot or will not meet her requests entirely, she will begin the process of separation.

EXAMPLE #2: Nathan Stepping Up

The following is an example of a man named Nathan who uses POET to deepen intimacy in his *self-relationship* and identify boundaries to strengthen and support Level Three, friendship, with his adult children.

THE SCENARIO:

Nathan has two adult children and three grandchildren. His oldest daughter lives out of state, and his son lives 45 minutes away.

Nathan always imagined being close to his grandchildren, but since his wife, Kathy, died three years ago, he hasn't had as much engagement with his children or his grandchildren. His wife had always been the one to initiate contact and make plans to see them.

When his oldest grandson turned 12 last week, Nathan woke up to how quickly they are growing. He doesn't want to miss the opportunity to form bonds with his grandchildren and has decided to use POET to gain some clarity.

PRESENCE – P

Nathan begins by presencing the situation:

> *"I only have contact with my kids and grandkids once a month, maybe less. When we talk, it's usually because one of us got lucky enough to catch the other on the phone for a quick hello."*

Next, Nathan presences his struggle, the vacillation between his hope and fear (generally outside of one's personal power):

> *"I struggle with how little I see the grandkids. I hope they will have lots of good memories of me and know how much I love them. Since Kathy died, I now fear they won't have as many memories with me or know how much I love them."*

Next, Nathan presences his desire. Remember that desire in the context of POET will encompass both the hope and fear and is generally a shift from what is outside of one's personal power to what is presently within it:

> *"No matter how my kids and grandkids interpret their time with me, I want to be the kind of dad and grandpa that shows up and engages consistently."*

OWNING REALITY WITH COMPASSION – O

Here, Nathan uses supportive phrases to make space for the reality of his struggle and desire.

- *"No wonder I haven't engaged with my kids or grandkids as often; I have always relied on my wife to make the plans.*
- *"Even though I have relied on her and haven't stepped up into that role yet, I deeply and completely honor and respect myself."*
- *"I give myself permission to learn how to show up consistently."*

As he says the last supportive phrase, a thought bubbles up:

"If I step up, Kathy will never come back."

He feels a lump rise in his throat and tears well in his eyes.

He now sees that a part of him, however illogical, has unconsciously believed that if Kathy could see how much he needs her, she would somehow be able to return to his life.

EXPLORATION – E

He takes this thought into exploration.

"If I step up, Kathy will never come back."

"How do I treat myself when I'm believing this thought?"

"I act incapable, like I don't know how to be the dad or grandpa I want to be. I don't take much initiative, and I feel like a victim of circumstance, believing I'm no good at nurturing the family. I reinforce the story that women are

> *better than men at maintaining family ties. I limit myself and what I can create with my kids and grandkids."*

Nathan takes the thought, *"If I step up, Kathy will never come back,"* and flips it around to view its opposites:

- *"If I don't step up, Kathy will never come back."*
- *"If I do step up, Kathy will come back."*

It's as if a switch flips, and the world suddenly brightens.

One of the things Nathan cherished about Kathy was her profound appreciation for their family. Now, he sees that by caring for his children and grandchildren, he enlivens something that holds immense value for them both.

Engaging with his family feels like breathing life into Kathy's memory and maintaining something they both hold dear. Contemplating it from this perspective fills him with a sense of closeness to her.

TAKE ACTION – T

Nathan can now see that he has been in a flight response regarding how to engage with his kids and grandkids since Kathy died. He sees that for him to be the father and grandfather he wants to be, he needs to step up, see himself as capable, and step toward engagement with his family. He sees that doing this will bring him back to his center, the truth of his desire.

He creates a plan. The specifics include:

- Scheduling two Zoom calls or in-person visits every month with each of his kids and their spouses. These calls will include time to talk with the grandkids.
- Every month, he will write one letter to each grandchild. He will include a memory or picture that also includes Kathy.
- He will send each grandchild a gift once a quarter, giving them something that connects to what he is learning about them through his time with them.
- He will plan one trip each year that he will initiate and pay for. These trips will include invitations to both of his kids and their families.

Along with this plan, Nathan hires a personal coach to support him in enacting his plan and to help him create a community with others outside of his family. He also joins an online grief group where he can get support to continue working through the experience of Kathy's death.

EXAMPLE #3: Michelle and Eric Using POET Individually and Together

EXAMPLE OF POET IN ACTION AT LEVEL 4 – INTIMACY

In this example, Michelle uses POET to strengthen intimacy in her self-relationship. She then extends the practice into her relationship with her business partner, Eric. Together, they use

POET to develop more intimacy (engagement with the truth) in their relationship as business partners.

THE SCENARIO:

Eric and Michelle are business partners. They have been running a company together for 15 years. While the company has made enough to give each of them a monthly paycheck that covers basic living costs, there is little extra to spare, and the constant sense of wondering whether there will be enough each month can feel unnerving.

While they both feel responsible for being financially successful, Eric is more likely to panic about whether or not they will have enough for their monthly paychecks. Michelle often helps support Eric by hearing him out and reminding him how, even though it's scary, they've been able to make payroll every month for 15 years now.

This month, they are lower than usual on cash flow. Eric wonders if they will need to pull money from other places to cover payroll. While Michelle sees the potential issue, she has used her extra time from a slower month to work on innovating one of their products and taking a marketing course. She also knows that they have some assets they can sell to get them through a rough few months if needed.

One day, Michelle senses that Eric is anxious. She asks if there's something she can do to support him. He mentions his financial anxiety about the upcoming month. He shares his fears and expresses concern that they do not have a plan. Michelle feels defensive that her efforts to innovate and learn more about marketing are not being considered.

In response to Michelle's struggle of wanting her efforts to be seen and acknowledged but not feeling like they are, her sense of self collapses. She then moves toward Eric energetically to engage him, hoping to receive validation for her efforts. She says that she does have a plan. At this point, Michelle has swayed out of her center and into the fawn response.

When Eric begins questioning her about her plan, she gives a general description, reinforcing her belief that her product innovation and marketing education will create more financial movement.

Eric wants specific numbers, and she begins to feel smaller and smaller as she waits for him to acknowledge her efforts. When Eric asks another question about the specifics of her plan, she retorts in an accusing tone that she has a plan, and it seems like he is the one without one.

Michelle says she needs space. She then leaves the room and takes some time to work with the POET process.

PRESENCE – P

Michelle begins by presencing her struggle, including the vacillation between her hope and fear, both of which are outside of her personal power.

> *"I can see that I've been fawning, trying to get Eric to acknowledge and appreciate my efforts. My hope is that he will see my efforts*

and vision and feel less anxious. I believe that if this happens, we can create a successful business. I fear that if he doesn't see my efforts and vision, he will continue to feel anxious, and without his support, we will not be able to create a successful business.

Michelle then presences her desire, which encompasses both the hope and fear and is within the realm of her personal power:

"Whether or not Eric can see my efforts and vision, and whether or not he feels anxious, I want to believe in myself and do everything I can to create a thriving business."

OWNING REALITY WITH COMPASSION – O

Here, Michelle uses supportive phrases to make space for reality, including her struggle and desire:

- *"Even though Eric got fixated on the numbers when I tried to support him emotionally, I deeply and completely respect him."*
- *"I give Eric permission to feel anxious as long as he needs to."*
- *"Just because a part of me buys into the story that I'm not doing enough doesn't mean I'll always buy into that story."*
- *"This is what it is like to be in the middle of growing my confidence."*
- *"No wonder I want to withdraw and do my work secretively when I don't feel seen."*

The last supportive phrase brought up a familiar feeling and a memory.

Michelle was raised in a high-demand religion with specific stories about what she needed to believe if she wanted to maintain a connection with her spiritual source. As a teenager, she started questioning the narrative. When she began asking questions, friends and family started pushing back. She noticed that rather than continue to share her new vision of spirituality, she withdrew, living most of her spiritual life in secret.

Michelle now sees the thought that has been hiding: *"What if I am wrong?"*

Like her quest to find an authentic spirituality, finding an authentic expression of being in business has been a journey. While asking hard questions about what will truly serve both her customers and herself has been enlightening, it has also felt scary. As she adopts new ideas, possibilities, and ways of thinking, she wonders, *"What if I am wrong?"*

EXPLORATION – E

She takes the thought, *"What if I am wrong?"* into exploration and asks the following question:

"What happens when I believe the thought, 'What if I am wrong?'"

> *"I feel scared and small. I want to hide. I want to explore and experiment in secret. I believe that I need Eric and others to validate my vision and actions. I feel depressed. I lose touch with myself."*

Michelle then mirrors the thought, *"What if I am wrong?"* by labeling its opposites:

- *"What if I am not wrong?*
- *"What if others are wrong?"*

She snaps back into the center of her relationship with herself. She feels the power of her efforts and work. She sees how amazing it is that she has run a business for 15 years that could pay her every month. She acknowledges an expanded vision has begun to materialize as she imagines growing the business and helping more people.

TAKE ACTION – T

Michelle sets a new intimacy boundary with herself. The boundary is that instead of letting anyone's anxiety, including Eric's or her own, be an indicator of her efforts or her ability to be successful, she will continue to trust her desires. She will use logical measures to assess if her efforts are working to create a business that is both successful and aligned with what she wants, and she will adjust as needed.

MICHELLE AND ERIC ENGAGE IN THE POET PROCESS TOGETHER

The next day, Eric and Michelle revisit their conversation together.

PRESENCE – P

Eric says, *"It felt really hard to hear you say that I was the one without a plan. You seemed mad at me, and I felt sad. What was the hardest part about that conversation for you?"*

Michelle shares, *"The hardest part was hearing you say that I didn't have a plan and then feeling pressure when you continued asking for specific numbers about my plan, even after I told you that I didn't know the numbers."*

Eric then asks if Michelle would listen to him and do reflective listening. Here, he is sharing a need to be heard and asking for consent from Michelle. She agrees.

Eric presences more details about his struggle. He shares how stressful it was to get the message from Michelle that he was doing something wrong by asking her questions. He explains that he was beginning to doubt himself and wondered if he should ignore the topic or stop asking questions.

Michelle reflects Eric's experience back to him: *"It sounds like it was hard to ask me details about my plan and then get a message from me that you were doing something wrong and should stop asking me questions."*

"Yes, it was so painful and confusing," Eric responds. *"I really want to know that it is safe for me to ask questions and talk about any topic related to our business."*

OWNING REALITY WITH COMPASSION – O

Michelle responds, *"It makes so much sense to me that you want to feel safe asking questions and know that no topic is off the table. I am so sorry that I made you feel like it wasn't safe to ask questions."*

Here, Michelle owns Eric's desire with compassion. She also owns the way that she contributed to his lack of safety.

Eric relaxes. *"Thank you," he says. "That feels helpful. And I can see how, when I am anxious, my questions might feel a bit relentless."*

Here, Eric owns with compassion that his anxiety can impact his ability to attune to Michelle.

Michelle feels relieved. *"Yes, they did. Thank you for seeing that."*

EXPLORATION – E

Next, Michelle goes a little deeper and begins to explore why she felt threatened by Eric's continued questions.

> *"I notice that sometimes I believe that I'm responsible for your anxiety. I doubt whether I'm doing enough, and I assume that if I did more, you would feel more relaxed. I think that is why, when I am trying to support you emotionally, and then in that same conversation, you begin asking questions about my numbers in the business, I get all tangled up. I start to believe that if I could reassure you with numbers, you wouldn't feel anxious, but I can't do that, and I begin to feel pressure and fear."*

Eric says, *"It sounds like you sometimes believe that you are not doing enough and that you are responsible for my anxiety."*

"Yes, that sums it up," Michelle responds.

They now see two stressful thoughts contributing to Michelle's struggle with Eric:

- *"I am not doing enough."*
- *"I am responsible for Eric's anxiety."*

Together, Michelle and Eric look at the opposites of these thoughts:

- *"Michelle is doing enough."*
- *"Michelle is not responsible for Eric's anxiety."*

They use logic to look at the reality of what Michelle is doing, which is enough from both of their perspectives. They also address the reality that if Michelle is doing enough, then Eric's anxiety is not about how much Michelle is or isn't doing. Michelle feels relieved and notices a lightening of the heaviness in her chest.

Next, Eric takes time to go a little deeper, exploring the source of his anxiety:

> *"I don't know how we are able to make it work each month. Somehow, it just does. Even though I'm grateful that it does, it also feels outside of my control. That feels scary, and when I feel scared, I fantasize about having more. I imagine that if we had more money, I would feel more in control and wouldn't have to wonder whether or not we're going to make it month-to-month. When I feel the panic rise, I start to believe that the business will fail. I think I'm not doing enough to grow it or keep it going, and I imagine that it will always feel like a struggle.*

Eric has identified three stressful thoughts connected with his anxiety:

- *"The business is going to fail."*
- *"I'm not doing enough in the business."*
- *"This will always be a struggle."*

Together, Michelle and Eric flip these thoughts into their opposites:

- *"The business is not going to fail."*
- *"Eric is doing enough in the business."*
- *"This will not always be a struggle."*

They discuss the reality that they have great products that help people, the problems they solve will continue needing solutions, and they have received positive feedback from their customer reviews.

While they both desire to be more profitable, Eric begins to see that the path to that happening is to go through precisely what they are going through today.

They are both continuing to learn and are both engaged in product development. Eric sees how this will allow them to help more people at a lower cost to the customer and with a higher profit margin for the business. Eric begins to see his work in a new light. What looked like a struggle yesterday now looks like a normal part of developing himself and growing a business.

TAKE ACTION – T

Eric and Michelle feel a renewed connection to themselves, each other, and their business. They set up a time to discuss the details of a financial plan to get them through this next phase of their business. They recommit to the work they are both doing in product development, and they decide to set up a meeting with a new marketing company to help them reach more customers.

SUMMARY

The POET process is an intimacy development practice designed to support you in fulfilling intimacy needs.

To effectively engage POET, the first three levels of relationship needs must be sufficiently established.

To engage POET with another person, you must both consent, and both be able to do your part of the process.

Similar to mastering a body practice, such as yoga, there are layers of POET that can take years to master, but even a little bit of work can make a big difference.

Just like you need yoga or another sport to achieve body mastery, an intimacy development process such as POET is essential for developing your ability to engage and experience more advanced levels of intimacy.

The goal of intimacy is engagement with the truth. In intimacy development, you expand your capacity to "be with" what is happening so that you can maintain or realign with center.

Center represents alignment with the truth of who you are, the truth of your relationships, and the truth of your desires.

Aligning with center requires a clear understanding of logic and emotion and how the two work together.

If POET or any other intimacy development practice ever threatens your safety, step back, take a break, or get the support you need. Always attend to the lower three levels of the relationship hierarchy when needed.

Chapter 16
RELATIONSHIP NEED - LEVEL FIVE

At the pinnacle of the pyramid is relationship need Level Five—EXPANSION.

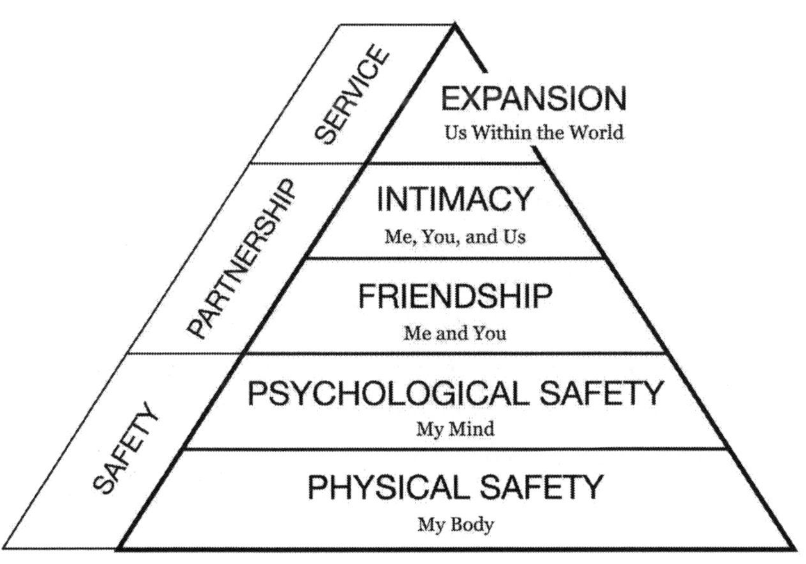

Figure 12 – The Hierarchy of Relationship Needs (Bauer, 2021)

The subtitle for expansion is "Us Within The World." Expansion represents the realm of service and is sourced from five specific qualities—*alignment, flow, abundance, passion, and creativity.*

At this level, service arises naturally from alignment with values, connection to flow states, access to a channel of abundance, and the experience of authentic passion.

In the fulfillment of expansion, giving and receiving flow effortlessly, amplifying and expanding the experience of aliveness.

Regarding expansion in self-relationship, here, truths of the self, reclaimed during intimacy, are shared with the world. With more access to more parts of yourself, you can both give and receive from a more complete, centered, and authentic version of who you are.

Regarding expansion in relationship with another, consider the metaphor of figure skating. The pinnacle of fulfillment for many figure skating pairs is to take what they have created together and share it with the world, showcasing their skills, inspiring others, and receiving a witness to their athletic dance.

All forms of relationship expansion follow the same pattern, resulting in both the individual parts of the whole sharing more truth with the world and the relationship offering a more expanded contribution of what's possible together.

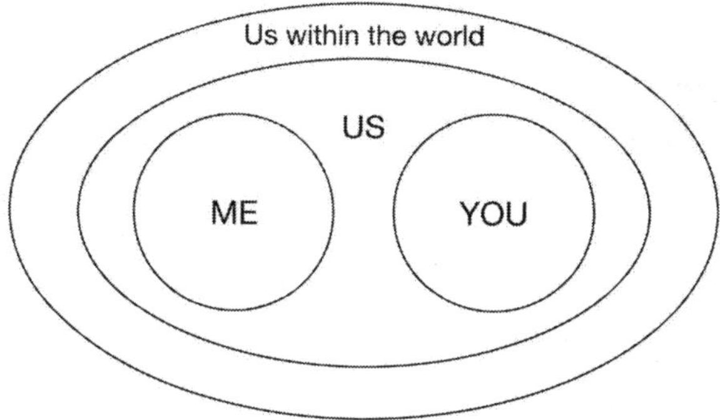

Figure 13 - The Orientation of Expansion

THE QUALITIES OF EXPANSION

The five qualities of expansion are *alignment, flow, abundance, passion, and creativity.*

Alignment

Alignment is a prerequisite for expansion, and its shape begins to clarify during intimacy development.

Alignment includes a harmonizing of the opposites.

Alignment in a yoga pose includes harmonizing the right and left, the front and back, and the top and bottom of the body.

Alignment in collaborating with another includes harmonizing logic and emotion, both people's needs, listening and talking.

Alignment is not about right and wrong or good and bad. It is not about morality or immorality. For example, you are not morally wrong if you are misaligned in a yoga pose. You are simply not yet aligned.

If, in a relationship, you are misaligned with commitment, you are not good or bad; you are simply not yet aligned with commitment, and, therefore, unable to express or expand commitment. When alignment with the desired outcome begins to take shape, it will start to express itself in form.

In yoga, if you want to do a pigeon pose, you must first align your body parts with the pigeon pose expression. Once aligned, you can expand into a full expression of the posture. Here your body can give and receive in ways that were not previously available. For example, in a pigeon pose, you can give yourself a hip stretch and receive more open hips.

The same is true as one moves through the levels of relationship development. The first three levels prepare you for alignment. Next, In level four—intimacy—you clarify the desired outcome and take action to engage alignment with that desired outcome, also known as center.

In relationship work, the desired outcome might be the experience of more appreciation, fun, commitment, sexual pleasure, emotional closeness, or understanding. Once aligned with that desire, you can express and expand that alignment, giving and receiving in new ways.

Flow

Flow is the experience of being so fully immersed in the moment that you begin to experience a sense of oneness between your internal and external world. Here, your mind, body, and environment work together, supporting an experience of ease as you expand and express what you have aligned with.

In flow, the opposites lose their distinction as they support each other in wholeness: effort and non-effort merge into one. You are *doing* at the same time you experience the *doing* as happening to you. Giving and receiving become two sides of the same coin as you receive at the same time you give and give at the same time you receive.

Abundance

Abundance includes having plenty of resources to meet your needs and desires and establishing an overflow from which you can give.

As you progress through intimacy, establishing higher and higher levels of alignment, you will encounter the vibrant sense of aliveness that results from closeness with your true self and others. This aliveness generates flow states from which resources can emerge.

This emergence of resources is reflected in three ways: having, doing, and being. Having refers to what you can have, doing refers to what you can do, and being refers to who you can be.

For example, you can have time, money, health, support, commitment, love, knowledge, and skills. Things you can do include working, traveling, relaxing, relating, exercising, committing, caring, conversing, parenting, and reading. Who you can be include kind, generous, joyful, honest, loyal, supportive, safe, loving, engaged, curious, attentive, or free.

Through alignment, you receive resources—having, doing, and being. In expansion, you channel the overflow of these resources into giving. Here, you can help others to have more, do more, and be more, just as others have helped you to have more, do more, and be more.

Passion

Passion is the experience of unmasked desire.

Passion may be viewed as threatening, dangerous, or harmful at lower levels of the hierarchy. That is because when true desires are less conscious, attempts to get them met might burn out of control as you seek to manifest your desires while simultaneously trying to hide them.

However, at the level of expansion and following the establishment of the four prior relationship needs, passion is not something to be feared.

In passion, you begin to see that your desires, while reflected in many external forms, are always sourced from within.

Passion reminds you that genuine desire is synonymous with genuine self, your true desires are synonymous with your true self, and the real desires of your relationships are synonymous with the real identity of that relationship.

Creativity

Creativity is using imagination and possibility to breathe life into new ideas, solutions, perspectives, expressions, and combinations of desire.

Creativity is the vehicle through which expansion and evolution emerge, bursting forth in a bright light or quietly creating change.

Years ago, I attended a lecture by a prominent astrophysicist. During the Q&A session, an audience member inquired about how we could gauge the nearing accessibility of space travel for the average person. The scientist responded that we would see it appear in the arts more. He continued to elaborate that, from his perspective, the arts and imagination lead the way.

Creativity takes our desires and makes something of them, expressing them into form through artwork, invention, business, dialogue, and relationships.

Every relational advancement is born and nurtured through the creative process. Whether it unfolds consciously or unconsciously, creativity is both a requirement and an outcome of expansion.

CHALLENGES TO EXPANSION

The following are challenges that can block, slow down, or halt expansion generally or regarding specific attributes of expansion:

- **Blind spots, ruptures, weakness, or lack of maintenance** in the first four levels of the hierarchy. If safety, friendship, and intimacy, needs are not adequately addressed or strengthened, they can hinder the integration of Level Five. Continuously attending to the basics is essential for the healthy support of all five levels.

- **Believing that service is** synonymous with obligation, martyrdom, scarcity, or lack.

- **Attempting expansion without** sufficient reception of resources. The term "premature scaling" is used to indicate that a business is expanding too quickly. Whether in business or relationships, premature expansion can impede progress.

- **When expansion does begin**, continually receiving resources is necessary to sustain giving as well as prevent burnout and fatigue. In the realm of expansion, receiving resources is equally important to giving them. Believing that giving is better than receiving can slow down or halt expansion opportunities.

- **Lack of coaching, mentorship, or support**. Just like professional athletes benefit from skilled coaches, any area of expansion can benefit from mentors, coaches, and supportive networks. Relationships that expand without adequate support can start to feel starved of the resources they need to flourish and thrive.

- **Misconceptions and unexplored fears** can stall the fulfillment of expansion. These fears generally stem from unconscious blind spots in the lower levels that become apparent when the weight of expansion is placed on the pyramid. Some examples of these fears include:

- Believing that expansion means neglecting the fundamentals of relationship development.
- Fearing that expansion is risky or dangerous even when you are safe and lower-level boundaries are secured.
- Thinking that it is best to keep your successes to yourself, associating expansion with bragging, lacking humility, or being conceited.
- Fearing that those you associate with will not understand or will judge you or reject you if you engage in expansion.
- Believing that expansion represents your inherent worth or value rather than an opportunity that arises at a particular stage of relationship development.
- Thinking that you must expand according to someone else's view of expansion.

You're almost to the end...If you like this book I would love to hear about it!

I love to read your reviews!

To leave a review log into your Amazon account, search the book, or click on your order, and leave a review on the book's page.

Thank you for letting me be a part of your journey!

Jenny Morrow

Chapter 17
LEVEL FIVE BOUNDARIES

EXPANSION BOUNDARIES

Boundaries executed during expansion support all five levels of relationship needs. At the level of expansion specifically, boundaries support the giving and receiving of resources in accordance with alignment, flow, abundance, passion, and creativity.

BOUNDARIES THAT SUPPORT EXPANSION GENERALLY:

- **Continue to monitor** the needs of hierarchy Levels one through Four, immediately addressing and repairing any ruptures at those levels.

- **Employ boundaries that** facilitate an ongoing balance between giving and receiving. Learn how to recognize when the outflow exceeds the inflow and vice versa.

- **Seek support and guidance** from third parties whenever necessary. This support may include advisors, mentors, coaches, therapists, books, educational programs, and other relevant resources.

BOUNDARIES THAT SUPPORT ALIGNMENT:

- **Remember that alignment**, while having a general framework, also encompasses elements distinctive to each person. For example, there are universal components to aligning oneself with commitment. Simultaneously, each individual's alignment with commitment will have unique features to its expression. Drawing a parallel to yoga, consider the pose "downward dog." Generally, it looks a certain way, and there is a standard pattern of body positioning to achieve and maintain the pose. However, individual bodies vary, and each person aligning with downward dog will have a unique expression of the pose.

- **Learn cues to help you** recognize instances of misalignment, and don't dismiss these cues. If something isn't lining up, establish a personal boundary that prevents you from constructing narratives to evade the discomfort of the unknown. Practice being with the unknown, balancing your openness to new information with your ability to be patient. If there is a way to gather more information, engage a willingness to be in the process of data gathering and exploration for as long as needed.

- **Remember that misalignment is not** an indicator of whether or not you should be in a particular relationship. It is not uncommon for people to believe that if they experience conflict or differences with someone, it must mean that they are misaligned and should end the relationship with that person. The reality is that every close relationship, including your relationship with yourself, will experience conflict and differences. Whether or not you want to do the work of using those conflicts and differences as an opportunity to get realigned with yourself or another is up to you. If safety and friendship are already established, you can apply the POET process to areas of conflict and differences to get more understanding, realign, and become available for expansion again.

- **Remember that alignment**, whether in a self-relationship or a relationship with another, cannot be forced. If there is a block in assessing, creating, or maintaining alignment, get support, practice patience, and take breaks as needed.

BOUNDARIES THAT SUPPORT FLOW:

- **Deliberately apply focus to** the edges of your intimacy capacity or competencies. Here, you employ learning. With practice and time, what previously demanded conscious effort becomes second nature. At this stage, you begin to harmonize your unconscious and conscious processes, allowing opportunities for flow states to arise. Suppose you aspire to become an exceptional listener and truly attune to others. Begin by acquiring deep listening skills and practice them consciously, stretching the edges of your current capacity. Observe as the ability to enter flow states in the realm of listening begins to emerge over time.

- **Practice harmonizing the opposites.** During intimacy development, you create a more neutral state of mind by equalizing the value of all opposites. During expansion, you use the foundation of that equality and the harmony of opposites to support flow states. If you desire to become a better listener, you also learn to receive listening, as receiving attentive listening grows your capacity to give it.

- **Mitigate distractions** and manage advanced levels of self-care. While they often feel effortless, flow states require a high level of attention and focus. For this reason, it is essential to mitigate distractions and maintain advanced levels of self-care. Maintaining consistent flow states in relationships is much more likely when you have created spaces free from distractions and are healthy, well-rested, sufficiently fed, and emotionally and cognitively available. I often remind clients, "The closer you get to who you want to be, the more essential boundaries become." Those who fulfill all five levels of relationship needs have the greatest capacity to set and maintain the most clear, consistent, and aligned boundaries with themselves and others.

- **Trust yourself.** When you reach Level Five—expansion—much of the preparatory work has already happened. Picture yourself as the lead in a play. You've diligently rehearsed your lines and attended all the rehearsals. Now it is time to perform, and your main job is to trust your preparation and enjoy the journey.

- **Let go of the how.** When in the flow, set intentions and let go of the how. At these levels, the mind is a supportive part of the process, not the whole process. In expansion, you are working with influences beyond the individual mind or the relationship's mind. Here, giving and receiving extends to include the entire world and beyond.

BOUNDARIES THAT SUPPORT ABUNDANCE:

- **Work through limiting beliefs** about resources and giving and receiving. For example, if you believe that productive people don't have time to meditate, explore your assumptions about time. If you think that only greedy people have high levels of wealth, explore your beliefs about money.

- **Observe the ways you** receive and allocate resources. Be attentive to subtle changes. Learn how to pivot and move when there are genuine shifts in your values. Doing this allows you to maintain your integrity and alignment regarding the reception and channeling of resources.

- **Stay open to discovering the source of abundance** and your nature in relationship to abundance. For example, when you believe financial abundance is sourced from hard work, look at the evidence. Notice how many hard-working people do not experience financial abundance and vice versa.

- **Stay focused on the long game.** Rather than acquiring just to acquire or giving just to give, stay focused on how giving and receiving can happen in relation to flow states, authentic values, and through the channel of abundance. This requires a willingness to practice new mindsets and approaches, make mistakes, continue learning, and remember that today is simply the outcome of your past process. Work with it, not against it, using the truth of where you are today to propel you into the potential of tomorrow.

BOUNDARIES THAT SUPPORT PASSION:

- **Take time to revel in** the experience and fulfillment of desire. Delight in the fresh peach you are eating. Engage with the blooming buds in your garden. Inhale the crisp fall air as you walk through the crunchy leaves. Soak in the warmth of your partner's skin as you cuddle up at night. Open to the joy of seeing your friend's bright blue eyes, and observe how your heart sings when you work well with your team. Ultimately, you can do this whether you are experiencing the desire in your mind or in manifested reality.

- **Access passion by exposing** yourself to places where your true desires can be lived out. For example, if you have a passion for money and open conversations but have been taught that talking about money is taboo, begin to expose yourself to places that speak about money openly and honestly. This could be fields of study, books, groups, or coaching. If you do not yet know places that could integrate your desires, imagine them.

- **Affirm and relate to** your passions and desires as absolutes. Remember that unmasked desires are reflections of the real you. They are not something you need to get from outside of yourself.

For example, rather than, *"I need you to appreciate me so that I know I am lovable,"* or *"I need you to commit to me so that I can see I am worthy of commitment,"* the orientation of expansion is as follows:

In self-relationship:

- *I am appreciative of myself and of those who support that appreciation*
- *I am committed to myself and to those who support that commitment.*

In relationship with another:

- *We are appreciative of ourselves, each other, our relationship, and of those who support our appreciations.*
- *We are committed to ourselves, each other, our relationship, and to those who support our commitments.*

BOUNDARIES THAT SUPPORT CREATIVITY:

- **Engage in practices that allow** you to be playful with the senses. This could include attending a cheese tasting, a painting class, getting a massage, or cooking while mindfully smelling and tasting the flavors as you go.

- **Pay attention to creative** blocks and boredom. These may signal the need for rest, self-care, intimacy development, or added support. They may also flag an issue that needs attention at a lower level of the hierarchy.

- **Utilize courses, workbooks,** or mentorship designed to facilitate and enhance your ability to engage in a creative process.

- **Get specialized support** to facilitate creativity in the areas you are most interested in (such as communication, coding, baking, business design, dancing, business, or math).

- **Put yourself in places** to be inspired by others' creativity, including concerts, retreats, museums, nature, and exposure to architecture. Observe the creativity of those highly skilled in specific areas such as advanced parenting, conflict negotiation, or glass-blowing.

- **Utilize mentors, coaches,** teachers, mastermind groups, or accountability support to help you put your desires out into the world in form.

SERVICE

As you establish and fulfill expansion, the natural outcome is service.

It is crucial to comprehend that, within the realm of expansion, *service is never synonymous with sacrifice*. It does not entail obligation, martyrdom, or compromise. Instead, service is giving and receiving from alignment with an infinite well of abundance simply because it magnifies your joy and the experience of relationship fulfillment.

Service can take on as many forms and expressions as there are desires and passions. It is endless in nature and is not confined to traditional activities of what is considered service. Service can happen in any area of life, and it has nothing to do with whether or not you are paid.

Service, at the level of expansion, signifies an open channel of alignment, flow, abundance, passion, and creativity. Here, energy moves unencumbered.

The continuous interplay among giving and receiving at the level of expansion establishes an unending cycle of boundless potential and resource regeneration.

Chapter 18
NEXT STEPS

WHAT'S NEXT...

Congratulations! You have learned the Relationship Hierarchy of Needs and how to approach boundaries at each level.

One of the number one struggles I see when people are not getting the relationship results they want is that they are attempting to resolve relationship issues with boundaries that are not congruent to the level of relationship need they are working to address.

For example, if you are in a Level Two relationship struggle attempting to resolve the issue with Level Four boundaries, you will likely wonder why your attempts to fix the relationship issue are not working and why things might even be getting worse.

To resolve relationship issues and grow in relationship development, you must apply boundaries congruent to the level of relationship need you are working to fulfill, and you must satisfy preceding needs before you can attend to subsequent needs. No matter how badly you desire intimacy in a relationship, you cannot fulfill intimacy needs until physical safety, psychological safety, and friendship needs are met.

While you now have a comprehensive overview of the hierarchy, this is only the beginning! Just like mastering anything else, *Mastering Boundaries* and creating advanced relationships includes layers of learning, including the subtle layers of style and texture with which you imprint your unique fingerprint into boundary mastery.

If you plan to continue your boundary mastery journey, I have created a book bonus that includes:

- A 60-Min. video where I answer boundary questions from readers like yourself.

- Downloads of the charts and images used in this book, such as the Four Quadrants of Masking and the Advanced Relationship Blueprint.

- A library of Advanced Relationship videos from my husband, Bryce, and myself, delivered straight to your inbox, including:

- How To Share Your Needs In A Relationship
- Attachment Styles 101
- 3 Ways That Self Improvement is BLOCKING Your Growth

- Too Good To Leave & Too Bad To Stay. How To Navigate Relationship Ambivalence

To register for your free access to this book bonus go to:

www.jennymorrow.com/bookbonus

As soon as you register, you will emailed access to the entire book bonus features and video library.

I can't wait to support you as you continue your journey to master boundaries and learn how to create advanced relationships!

Thank you so much for letting me be a part of your journey!

REFERENCES

Bauer, Bryce. (2021). *The Hierarchy of Relationship Needs* [Chart]. Unpublished work. www.brycebauer.com

Karakurt, G., Whiting, K., Van Esch, C., Bolen, S., & Calabrese, J. (2016). *Couple Therapy for Intimate Partner Violence: A Systematic Review and Meta-Analysis. Journal of Marital and Family Therapy*, 42(4), 568-583. https://onlinelibrary.wiley.com/doi/10.1111/jmft.12178

Gottman Institute. (n.d.). *The Four Horsemen: Recognizing Criticism, Contempt, Defensiveness, and Stonewalling.* https://www.gottman.com/blog/the-four-horsemen-recognizing-criticism-contempt-defensiveness-and-stonewalling/

Hassan, S. (1988). *Combatting Cult Mind Control* (p. 114). ISBN 0-89281-243-5.

Freedom of Mind Resource Center. (n.d.). *BITE Model.* https://freedomofmind.com/cult-mind-control/bite-model/

Bowlby, J. (1969). *Attachment and Loss: Attachment* (Vol. 1). Basic Books.

Ainsworth, M. D. S. (1978). *Patterns of attachment: A psychological study of the Strange Situation.* Psychology Press.

Hazan, C., & Shaver, P. (1987). *Romantic love conceptualized as an attachment process. Journal of Personality and Social Psychology,* 52(3), 511-524. https://doi.org/10.1037/0022-3514.52.3.511

Chapman, G. (1995). *The Five Love Languages: How to Express Heartfelt Commitment to Your Mate.* Northfield Publishing.

Bill Moyers & Joseph Campbell. (1988). *Joseph Campbell and the Power of Myth: The Message of the Myth* [Video]. Retrieved from https://billmoyers.com/content/ep-2-joseph-campbell-and-the-power-of-myth-the-message-of-the-myth/

"List of Cognitive Biases." In *Wikipedia.* https://en.wikipedia.org/wiki/List_of_cognitive_biases. (Accessed October 3, 2023).

"Understanding and Overcoming Cognitive Distortions." *Psych Central.* https://psychcentral.com/lib/cognitive-distortions-negative-thinking. (Accessed October 4, 2023).

"List of Fallacies." (2023, October 19). In *Wikipedia.* https://en.wikipedia.org/wiki/List_of_fallacies.

Kahneman, D. (2011). *Thinking, Fast and Slow*. Farrar, Straus and Giroux.

Made in the USA
Middletown, DE
03 February 2025